Easy Stash Quilts

CAROL DOAK

Bothell, Washington

Credits

President . . . . Nancy J. Martin
CEO/Publisher . . . . Daniel J. Martin
Associate Publisher . . . . Jane Hamada
Editorial Director . . . . Mary V. Green
Design and Production Manager . . . . Cheryl Stevenson
Technical Editor . . . . Ursula Reikes
Copy Editor . . . . Tina Cook
Illustrator . . . . Laurel Strand
Photographer . . . . Brent Kane
Cover and Text Design . . . . Rohani Design
Proofreader . . . . Leslie Phillips

Martingale
& COMPANY

That Patchwork Place is an imprint of Martingale & Company.

MISSION STATEMENT

We are dedicated to providing quality products
and service by working together to inspire creativity
and to enrich the lives we touch.

Easy Stash Quilts
© 1999 by Carol Doak
Martingale & Company
PO Box 118
Bothell, WA 98041-0118 USA
www.patchwork.com

Printed in Hong Kong
04 03 02 01 00 99   6 5 4 3 2 1

Dedication

This book is dedicated to Helen Weinman, the owner of Heartbeat Quilts in Hyannis, Massachusetts. Helen is a dear friend who has made quilts for several of my books. She represents the many quilt shop owners who are always there for us with the latest quilt supplies and encouragement.

Acknowledgments

My heartfelt thanks and appreciation go to:

Ginny Guaraldi, Pam Ludwig, Ellen Peters, Helen Weinman, Sherry Reis, Carolyn McCormick, Ursula Reikes, and Colleen Pennington for accepting the opportunity to create wonderful stash quilts.

Ellen Peters and Judy Allen for their beautiful machine quilting.

Ursula Reikes for her dear friendship and skillful editing. She makes what I do such a joy!

My husband, Alan, for his support and encouragement.

My students, who constantly encourage and inspire new beginnings.

Library of Congress Cataloging-in-Publication Data

Doak, Carol.
    Easy stash quilts / Carol Doak.
        p.   cm.
    ISBN 1-56477-264-0
    1. Patchwork Patterns. 2. Quilting Patterns. I. Title.
TT835.D6284 1999
746.46—dc21   99-40528
                                                              CIP

Contents

Preface

How did I come to write a book about using stash fabrics? Once upon a time I designed a quilt, and one of the fabrics I needed was a tone-on-tone black. I didn't have enough yardage of any one tone-on-tone black in my fabric stash, so I went shopping but couldn't find what I wanted. I was excited about the quilt design and wanted to spend my time sewing rather than looking for this elusive fabric. My solution was to gather small pieces of tone-on-tone black fabrics from my stash and use them randomly. As I cut, I felt good about using my fabric stash. That good feeling inspired me to use the same approach for most of the other colors in my quilt.

Although I am an organized person by nature, when it came to sewing the piece, I made a commitment to pick up the next fabric in the stack and use it, without trying to match fabric placements. This forced the random placement of the different fabrics in each color group. Only when the next fabric was the same as the previous one

would I select an alternate fabric. The subtle differences between the fabrics added interest and excitement to my quilt. It was this excitement that led me to pursue the avenue of "stash quilts."

I named my quilt "Play the Sunset," after a scene in the movie *Mr. Holland's Opus*. In the movie, Richard Dreyfus portrays a high school music teacher who inspires a young student struggling to play the clarinet. When she reaches the point of giving up, he asks her to describe what she likes best about herself. She responds with a smile that it is her red hair, because her father said it reminded him of a beautiful sunset. Rather than struggle to read the notes, he encourages her to close her eyes, feel the music, and "play the sunset." The result is the beginning of a beautiful piece of music played with feeling and enjoyment. As I pieced this quilt, I felt a sense of relaxation and the freedom to just go with the flow as I picked up pieces of stash fabric. I had closed my eyes and played the sunset. The result was a beautiful quilt.

Introduction

Quilters have a love affair with fabric, and they collect fabrics wherever they go. A quilter's fabric collection is commonly called a "stash." In addition to large pieces of fabric, a quilter's stash usually includes fat quarters; 1/8-, 1/4-, and 1/3-yard cuts; and smaller pieces left over from previous projects. Many quilters often wonder what they can do with their ever-increasing collection. This book will show you how to use the fabrics in your stash to make fun and easy quilts.

My recipe for making a stash quilt is simple. Select one or two block designs, and assign a color and value to each patch in the blocks. Instead of using a single fabric for each color, select multiple fabrics from your stash that match the required color and value, and use them randomly in the assigned patch. There are three major benefits to this method:

◆ You'll use up a lot of small pieces from your stash, including all those fat quarters you've been accumulating.

- You won't have to do any fancy cutting. If you choose simple blocks for traditional piecing (or if you use my cutting technique for paper piecing), you won't have to do anything more complicated than rotary-cut squares, rectangles, and triangles.
- You will create a dramatic quilt with minimal effort.

In the first section of the book, "Fabric Stash Assignments," you'll learn how to assign color, value, and texture to your blocks and explore ways to gather fabrics from your stash. "Block Design Criteria" explains how to select blocks that are appropriate for stash quilts. Quick and easy rotary-cutting techniques are covered in "Rotary Cutting"; step-by-step directions for piecing blocks are included in "Block Assembly." Choose your favorite quilt from the photos, then follow the directions in "Quilt Projects." "Assembly and Finishing" leads you through the final steps.

So gather your fabrics and play the sunset to make fun and exciting stash quilts.

Tools and Supplies

The following items will assist you in making your stash quilts. Read the list carefully before assembling your supplies—if you don't plan to paper piece, you may not need every tool.

- Sewing machine that is tuned up and ready to fly.
- Sewing machine needles. For standard machine piecing, use a size 80/12 needle. For paper piecing, use a size 90/14 needle—it's larger than the 80/12 needle, and the bigger hole it creates makes it easier to remove the paper foundation.
- 6" and 12" Add-A-Quarter rulers for trimming fabric while paper piecing.
- Postcard for paper piecing. You'll fold the paper foundation against it before trimming. (See page 24.)

- Rotary cutter and mat.
- Rotary rulers in the following sizes: 6" × 6", 6" × 12", 12½" × 12½", and 6" × 24".
- Sandpaper grips to place along the edges of rotary rulers (and postcards, if you're paper piecing) to hold them in place.
- Fine silk pins without large heads for pinning fabric and securing paper foundations.
- Ruby Beholder®, value-finding tool for determining fabric value. (See page 7.)
- Small stick-on note pads for labeling fabric pieces with placement numbers and sizes.
- Scotch Brand Removable Tape for repairing torn paper foundations. (See page 26.)
- Calculator for determining how many pieces to cut from each fabric in a stash group.
- Colored pencils for indicating assigned colors.

Fabric Stash Assignments

To make a stash quilt, you need to assign a color and value to each patch in your block design. You can write the color assignments on a sample block, or use colored pencils to show the colors.

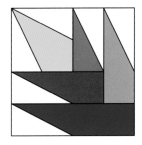

Assigned colors and values

Next, select a group of different fabrics for each color assignment. While each fabric in the group will be different, they should all share the same color and value, such as a variety of dark blues or a collection of light yellows. The fabrics in each group are used randomly in assigned spaces. The result is a quilt that has an organized scrap look.

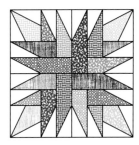

4 blocks worked in a variety of fabrics in the assigned colors and values.

An advantage of making stash quilts is that you don't need specific amounts of a particular number of fabrics for each color assignment. How many yellows you might use, and how much of each, depends on how many yellows you already have and the size of the pieces. You don't need to worry about running out of a particular fabric, because you can just add another fabric or cut more pieces from the other fabrics in that stash group as needed. With stash quilts, even a two-color design is visually exciting because each color assignment actually consists of several different fabrics.

Some quilts in this book call for a single fabric to be used in designated places. I refer to these as "constant" fabrics (see page 11).

COLOR

The primary colors are red, blue, and yellow. If you look at a color wheel, between the primary colors you'll find the secondary colors: orange (red and yellow), green (yellow and blue), and violet (blue and red). "Hue" is another word for color, and the terms are used interchangeably in this book.

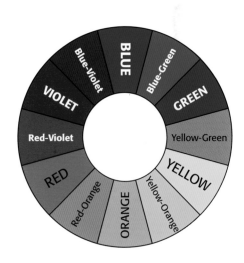

The greater the distance between two colors on the wheel, the greater the contrast between them. For example, the contrast between violet and green is stronger than the contrast between violet and blue because violet and green are farther apart on the color wheel. For high contrast, choose colors that lie opposite one another on the wheel. For low contrast, choose colors that lie near one other.

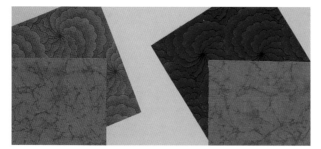

Low-contrast colors   High-contrast colors

When grouping prints for a particular color assignment, make sure the desired color predominates. Just because a fabric contains a green element doesn't mean it will look green when used in small amounts in a quilt. In the following example, the fabrics on the left contain too many large areas of other colors to be considered green. The fabrics on the right contain smaller amounts of other colors, but there is no doubt that these fabrics are light green. To see which color is dominant in a multicolor fabric, attach a small piece to a wall and step back about ten feet.

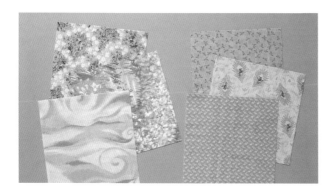

VALUE

"Value" is the relative darkness or lightness of a color. A black-and-white photograph shows only value. In order for a design to emerge in your quilt, you need to maintain a similar value within each stash group.

If you have a hard time separating value from color, you may want to try a value-finding tool like the Ruby Beholder. This red-tinted bar masks color and shows only value. In the photo above right, a piece of red-tinted plastic is placed over two fabric groups. Can you see how the values are different in the group on the left and similar in the group on the right? The fabrics on the left would not make a good stash group. The fabrics on the right would make an excellent stash group.

Poor stash group   Good stash group

While the Ruby Beholder is an invaluable tool, keep in mind that it doesn't work well with red fabrics. So be sure to carefully compare each red you're considering to others in the stash group to determine value.

Not only should the different fabrics in each stash group be of similar value and color, they should also blend with each other. No one fabric should stand out. Avoid fabrics with high-contrast elements when selecting stash groups, because they won't blend well. In the following example, the fabrics on the left contain high-contrast elements. When one of these fabrics is placed with fabrics of a similar color and value, the high-contrast elements stand out.

High-contrast fabrics   Mismatched fabrics

Contrast between stash groups is very important. The greater the value contrast, the more dramatic the finished quilt. In the following example, notice how the contrast between the light and medium fabrics is less dramatic than the contrast between the dark and light fabrics.

Mild contrast   High contrast

If you are seeking high contrast in your quilt, work with light stash groups and dark stash groups. For mild contrast, work either with light and medium stash groups, or with medium and dark stash groups. The following illustration shows the impact of value on a block design.

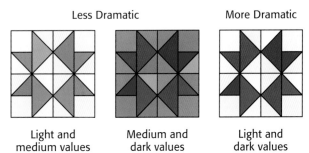

Less Dramatic   More Dramatic

Light and medium values   Medium and dark values   Light and dark values

TEXTURE

Another criterion for selecting fabrics is texture. Low contrast, limited colors, and a small-scale print create subtle texture. Medium contrast, multiple colors, and a large-scale print create intricate texture. Through use of texture, you can dramatically change the look of your quilt.

Tone-on-tone prints are examples of fabrics with subtle texture. If you were to look at a group of color- and value-matched tone-on-tone prints from ten feet away, it would be difficult to see a

difference in texture within the group. If you want the background of a block design to have subtle movement, tone-on-tone prints are an excellent choice. In the photo below, the fabrics on the left are examples of subtle texture.

A fabric that contains a variety of colors and design elements will have greater texture than a tone-on-tone print. The complex texture is evident when you view these fabrics from a distance. When creating a stash group of textured fabrics, be sure the assigned color and value is dominant.

Subtle texture   Lively texture

To illustrate how texture can affect a design, the following blocks were made using two different stash groups for the background pieces. In the block on the left, all the white background pieces have a subtle texture. In the block on the right, the white background fabrics show livelier textures. Can you see how the block on the left is clean and crisp, while the block on the right shows variety and movement?

STASH GROUPS

Now that we have discussed how color, value, and texture affect patchwork, we can discuss some of the choices you face when grouping stash fabrics. You can make each group similar in color, value, and texture, or you can stretch these criteria slightly to create more interest. When stretching the value, color, and texture within a stash group, don't do it with just one fabric, do it with several. If just one fabric is a stretch, it will stand out. Some avenues for stretching fabric stash assignments are:

◆ Assign more than one color to a stash group. A quilt of flowers could employ a variety of different pink and purple fabrics. Or, for a more complex look, you could try different colors of the same value, such as a broad color range of pastels for the flowers.

◆ Assign a wide value range to a stash group, such as medium to dark green. The wider the variance in value, the more complex the patchwork will appear.

◆ Use hues that are next to each other on the color wheel in a single stash group. A medium-value group that ranges from blue-green to blue-purple will generate more interest than a group of only medium blues.

◆ Assign a particular texture to a stash group, for example, all solids, checks, mini-prints, batiks, or large-scale prints.

Selecting fabric for a project is uncomfortable for some quilters. For others it is pure joy. The good news about gathering fabrics for stash quilts is that the end result does not rest solely on one fabric, but on the color, value, and texture of the stash group combinations. The number of fabrics in each stash group is flexible. More fabrics will create more interest and complexity. An average range for a stash group is six to twelve fabrics. I usually determine how many fabrics to include in a group based on how many fabrics I have in my stash that fit the assigned criteria, and how many pieces I need to cut. If the cutting list calls for one hundred squares, each 2½" × 2½", I would select ten fabrics and cut ten squares from each. You can adjust the number of fabrics up or down depending on the number of pieces needed for the block and the number of fabrics in your stash that fit the assigned criteria.

I don't concern myself at this point with the size of the pieces I'm selecting for the assigned stash group. Generally, the fabric pieces I choose are at least ⅛ yard to ¼ yard. My concern at this time is that the fabric pieces fit the criteria I have set for the stash group. When it's time to cut pieces from each stash group, if I find that one of the fabrics I've selected won't accommodate all the pieces I need to cut, I go to plan B and cut more pieces from one of the other fabrics in the group. Or, I can go to plan C and add additional fabrics that meet the stash group criteria. This is what is so super about stash quilts! You don't need to worry about running out of a particular stash fabric, because the recipe is flexible.

I'll use the following block to explain how to assemble stash groups. Say you want to use dark blue fabrics for the background, and light pink, medium pink, and light blue for designated design elements.

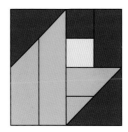

Begin by selecting dark blue background fabrics. If you want the differences between background fabrics to be subtle, choose fabrics that are similar in color and value. From your stash, gather either solid or tone-on-tone dark blue fabrics. Line up the fabrics so that a 2" strip of each is visible. I like to place them on the floor so I can stand back to get a better perspective. Confirm that the fabrics are similar in color and value, and make adjustments as needed.

If you want to add more interest to the background, include fabrics in slightly different hues of blue. The more hues of blue that you include, the more interesting the grouping will be. You can include fabrics that contain bits of other colors to make the background even more complex. Or, you can stretch the value range. My dark-blue stash group includes different hues of blue in a slightly stretched value range.

Gather light pink fabrics for the center squares. Line up these fabrics as before and stand back to confirm that they match. Again, they can be similar in color and value or stretched a bit in both areas. Because they will be next to each other in the block, place the light pink stash group next to the dark blue stash group to see how they will look together.

Next, gather the medium pink fabrics. These need to be darker than the light pinks and lighter than the dark blues because they will touch both. When a stash group needs to fall within a specific value range, I use a little trick. First, I find one fabric that fits the criteria. I call this my benchmark fabric. I then use this benchmark fabric as a guide for selecting other similar fabrics from my stash.

Line up the medium pink fabrics to confirm they are similar in color and value. Place this group between the dark blue and light pink fabrics to confirm that there is a difference between the three stash groups.

Gather your light blue fabrics. This time, the value needs to be lighter than both the medium pink and dark blue stash groups. Because the light blue and light pink fabrics do not touch each other in the block, their values don't need to be different from each other. They will also not be confused with each other because they are in fact different colors.

In the light blue stash group shown below, I used one of the fabrics twice—the solid fabric is actually the wrong side of one of the other fabrics.

Line up the fabrics and stand back to confirm that they are all light blue. Place this group next to the medium pink and the dark blue fabrics to confirm that there is a difference in value and color.

Place the four groups side by side to see how they will look together.

The block below was made from the four sample stash groups.

The best advice I can give you about gathering fabrics for each stash group is to trust your instincts. Don't talk yourself into a fabric and don't talk yourself out of one. Be flexible. Start with one fabric and add others within the desired color and value range. Once you've gathered a group of fabrics, it may be necessary to eliminate one because it stands out too much from the rest. Just keep playing until you are happy with your selections.

The large number of fabrics used in stash quilts make them very forgiving, so have fun with the fabric selection process.

CONSTANT FABRICS

I use "constant" to describe fabrics that are used consistently throughout a quilt. The border is an example of a constant fabric. Rather than choose four different border fabrics, one for each side, I prefer to use a single fabric. This creates an area where the eye can rest. A multicolor constant fabric can also be the basis for selecting the colors and values for the stash groups.

Another reason to use a constant fabric is to accent a particular area of a block, as with the gray fabric in the stars of "Play the Sunset" (page 28).

Block Design Criteria

Two machine piecing methods are used for the stash quilts in this book—traditional and paper foundation. The traditionally pieced block designs are made up of squares, rectangles, and triangles. The paper-pieced blocks include a variety of patchwork shapes, but the beauty of my paper-piecing method is that regardless of the finished patchwork shape, all the fabrics are cut into squares, rectangles, or triangles. This permits the use of quick-cutting techniques, such as cutting consistent shapes from several layers of fabric at once. If you want to limit the number of sizes to cut, use only one or two block designs made up of just a few pieces.

TRADITIONALLY PIECED DESIGNS

Ideal blocks for traditional piecing are those that have straight seams (no set-in seams), and relatively few pieces. Pieces are rotary cut to size plus $1/2$" for seam allowances. Select blocks that are easily divided by the grid on which the block is based. You want to be able to cut pieces in the increments found on rotary rulers. For example, a 9" block based on a 9-patch grid results in squares that finish to 3": 9" divided by 3 = 3".

The following table lists the finished-square size for both 9- and 16-patch grids. A blank indicates that the result is not an even ruler increment.

Remember to add $1/2$" seam allowances to the finished size of the pieces before cutting.

When searching for block designs to piece traditionally, keep the following criteria in mind. Blocks should:

◆ Contain only squares, rectangles, and/or half-square and quarter-square triangles.
◆ Have a limited number of pieces.
◆ Be easy to assemble, with no set-in seams.
◆ Be easy to make in the desired size, with easy-to-cut measurements.

Don't underestimate the potential of a simple block design made with a variety of fabrics.

Hour Glass   Colors assigned

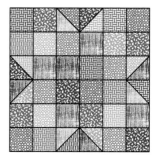

Stash fabrics used
for each color assignment
and blocks rotated.

Block Size	Finished size of square in a 9-patch grid	Finished size of square in a 16-patch grid
6"	2"	1½"
8"	—	2"
9"	3"	2¼"
10"	—	2½"
12"	4"	3"
15"	5"	3¾"

The following blocks would be appropriate for stash quilts. The single block design indicates the color and value assigned to the block. The group of four blocks shows how combining blocks and using stash fabrics creates interest. Stash fabric textures are not shown in the white background areas of these illustrations.

The following blocks create wonderful new designs when placed in four-block rotations.

Four-block rotation

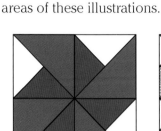

16-Patch
Windmill

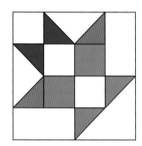

16-Patch
Baby Bunting

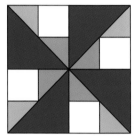

16-Patch
Brave World

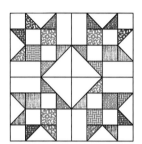

16-Patch
Autumn Tints

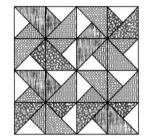

9-Patch
Tulip Time

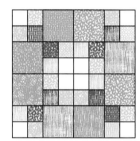

16-Patch
The Arkansas Cross Roads

You can also alternate two different blocks to create interesting quilts.

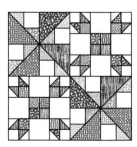
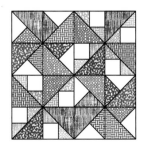

Alternating Block Designs

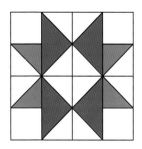

16-Patch
Ribbon Star

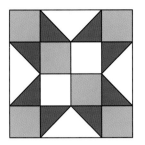

16-Patch
Indian Star

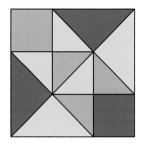

9-Patch
Daybreak

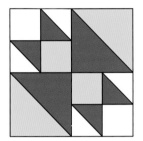

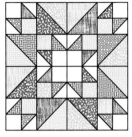

16-Patch
Hollis Star

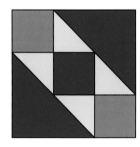

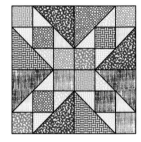

9-Patch
Attic Window Variation

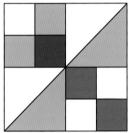

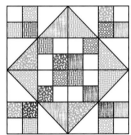

16-Patch
The Sickle

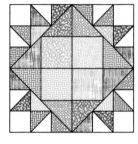

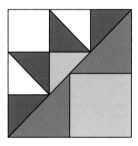

9-Patch
Friendship Block

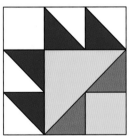

9-Patch
Maple Leaf (variation)

PAPER-PIECED DESIGNS

In paper piecing, oversize fabric pieces are sewn to a paper foundation in a numbered sequence. You'll notice that some of the paper-pieced blocks contain odd-shaped pieces. But instead of cutting fabric into awkward shapes, I simply rotary-cut oversize squares, rectangles, or triangles to accommodate the shapes in a block. This makes the cutting a breeze, which makes paper-piecing the perfect method for making intricate blocks. My previous books *Easy Machine Paper Piecing, Easy Paper-Pieced Keepsake Quilts,* and *Easy Mix & Match Machine Paper Piecing* feature a variety of 3" and 4" paper-piecing block foundations. If you want to use some of these blocks, I suggest you enlarge the designs to 5", 6", or 7" so the fabric pieces will be larger. (See page 23 for ways to reproduce paper foundations.)

9-Patch
Steps to the Altar

Some of the blocks in my previous books have pieced units. These are fabric pieces that you sew together prior to sewing them to the foundation. For your stash quilt, choose blocks without pieced units so you will not have to add this additional step.

There are many options for using just a few paper-pieced designs for a stash quilt. You can select one block for the entire quilt and use it repeatedly. Or, you can select two blocks and alternate them. Here are a few suggestions to ponder for future stash quilts.

 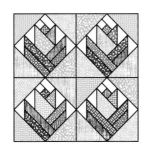

F4 from
Easy Machine Paper Piecing

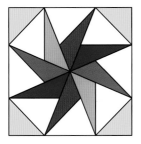 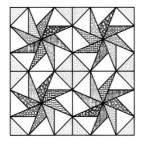

G35 from
Easy Mix & Match Machine Paper Piecing

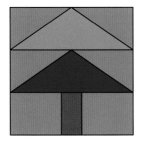 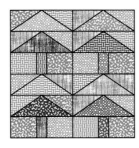

T12 from
Easy Paper-Pieced Keepsake Quilts

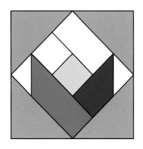 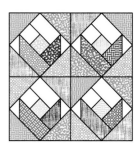

F27 from
Easy Paper-Pieced Keepsake Quilts

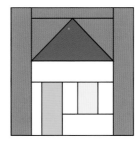 

P24 from
Easy Paper-Pieced Keepsake Quilts

 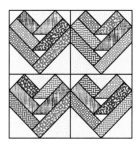

H12 from
Easy Paper-Pieced Keepsake Quilts

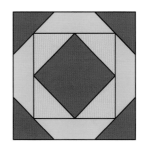 

G29 from
Easy Paper-Pieced Keepsake Quilts

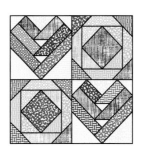 

Some alternating block suggestions

Another option is to use blocks that have a diagonal focus and use them in a four-block rotation. This produces some spectacular designs.

Diagonal Blocks

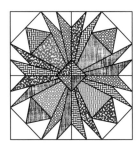

G19 from
Easy Paper-Pieced Keepsake Quilts

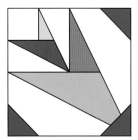

F9 from
Easy Machine Paper Piecing

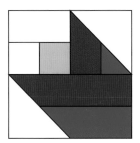
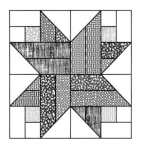

F31 from
Easy Paper-Pieced Keepsake Quilts

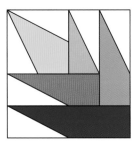
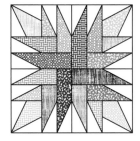

F39 from
Easy Mix & Match Machine Paper Piecing

G31 from
Easy Mix & Match Machine Paper Piecing

F32 from
Easy Mix & Match Machine Paper Piecing

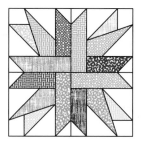
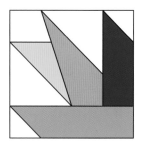

F38 from
Easy Mix & Match Machine Paper Piecing

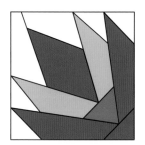

F43 from
Easy Mix & Match Machine Paper Piecing

Rotary Cutting

Now that you have selected your block design(s) and stash groups, it is time to begin cutting the fabric for the quilt. All the quilt blocks in this book are made from rotary-cut squares, rectangles, and triangles. I recommend that you always cut fabric for the borders, binding, and setting pieces first. That way, you can use the leftovers in one of your stash groups, if desired.

Strips

To make a clean cut across fabric and cut strips:

1. Fold the fabric in half with selvages matching. If you prefer, you can fold the fabric again for a shorter cutting distance.
2. Position the fabric on the cutting mat with the fold closest to you and uneven edges to the left. (Reverse these directions if you are left-handed.)

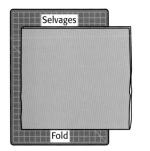 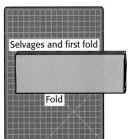

Fabric folded once   Fabric folded twice

3. Align the edge of a 6"-square ruler with the fold of the fabric. Butt a 6" × 24" ruler along the left of the square ruler.

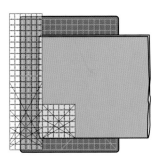

4. Remove the square, then rotary cut along the right-hand edge of the ruler to make a clean cut across the width of the fabric. Use firm, downward pressure as you cut, and be careful not to let the ruler slip out of position as you cut away from yourself.

5. Cut strips, aligning the clean-cut edge of the fabric with the ruler markings at the desired width.

◆ To cut squares from a strip, find the strip-width measurement on the ruler and align the mark with the short end of the strip. Cut. Continue cutting across the strip until you have the required number of squares.

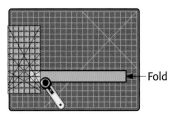

Fold

◆ To cut rectangles from a strip, align the desired mark on the ruler with the short end of the strip. Cut. Continue cutting across the strip until you have the required number of rectangles.

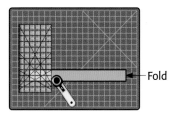

Fold

◆ To cut 2 half-square triangles (straight grain on the short side of the triangle), cut the required size square and then cut it once diagonally. Cut 1 square for every 2 half-square triangles required.

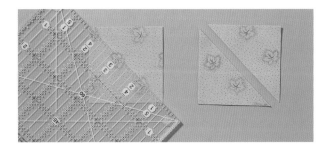

◆ To cut 4 quarter-square triangles (straight grain on the long side of the triangle), cut the required size square and then cut twice diagonally. Cut 1 square for every 4 quarter-square triangles required.

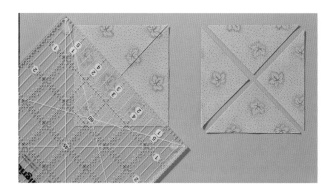

You may have irregular-shaped pieces in your collection that are just perfect for your stash groups. Simply stack several fabrics on top of each other and rotary cut squares from the stack. This approach can also be used to cut rectangles and triangles.

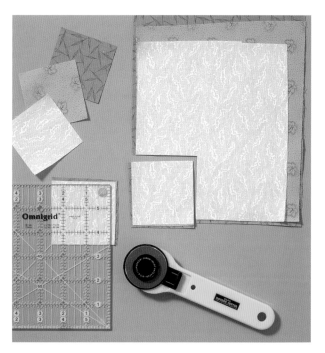

CUTTING FOR TRADITIONAL PIECING

Cut the fabric pieces to the finished size plus $1/2$" for seam allowances. Let's use the following 6" block to illustrate how to cut various shapes.

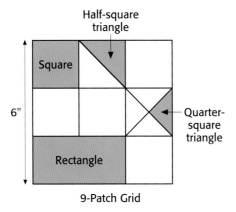

Half-square triangle

Square

6"

Quarter-square triangle

Rectangle

9-Patch Grid

For squares, add $1/2$" to the finished size of the square for seam allowances.

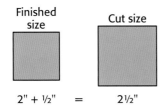

Finished size

Cut size

$2" + 1/2" = 2 1/2"$

For rectangles, add $1/2$" to the finished size of the rectangle for seam allowances.

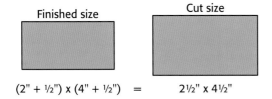

Finished size

Cut size

$(2" + 1/2") \times (4" + 1/2") = 2 1/2" \times 4 1/2"$

For half-square triangles (straight grain on the short side of the triangle), add $7/8$" to the finished size of the short side of the triangle for seam allowances. Cut a square that size and cut it once diagonally to make 2 half-square triangles.

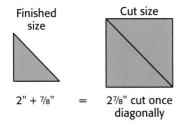

Finished size

Cut size

$2" + 7/8" = 2 7/8"$ cut once diagonally

For quarter-square triangles (straight grain on the long side of the triangle), add $1 1/4$" to the finished size of the long side of the triangle for seam allowances. Cut a square that size and cut it twice diagonally to make 4 quarter-square triangles.

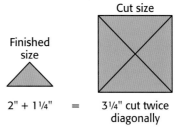

Finished size

Cut size

$2" + 1 1/4" = 3 1/4"$ cut twice diagonally

CUTTING FOR PAPER PIECING

Fabric pieces need to be larger than the area they will fill plus $3/4$" for seam allowances. Using a larger-than-normal seam allowance ensures that the piece will cover the patch area even if it slips a bit during sewing.

In this book, all the piece sizes and quantities are provided for each project. For your original projects, however, you should know how to determine cutting sizes. Remember, bigger is always better!

Start with piece #1. Place a gridded ruler over the area marked #1 in the same manner you will place fabric #1, to see how big the fabric piece needs to be, including a generous seam allowance. In the example below, you would cut a $2 1/2" \times 4"$ rectangle. In the photos, the areas being measured are shaded to make them more visible.

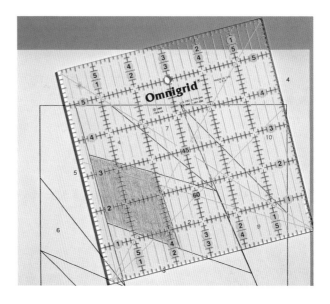

To measure subsequent pieces, place the $\frac{1}{4}$" line of the rotary ruler on the seam you will sew and let the rest of the ruler fall over the area being measured. Look at the ruler to see how big the piece needs to be, including a generous seam allowance on all sides. For piece #2, you would cut a $2\frac{1}{2}$" × $4\frac{1}{4}$" rectangle.

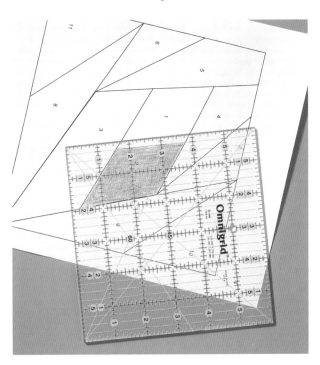

For half-square triangles (straight grain on the short side of the triangle), measure the short side of the triangle and add $1\frac{1}{4}$" to this measurement for seam allowances. Cut a square this size, then cut it once diagonally to make 2 half-square triangles.

Half-Square Triangles

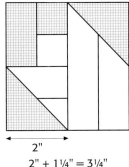

Block size is 4" finished.

2"

2" + $1\frac{1}{4}$" = $3\frac{1}{4}$"

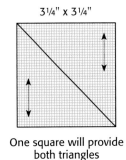

$3\frac{1}{4}$" x $3\frac{1}{4}$"

One square will provide both triangles for this block design.

For quarter-square triangles (straight grain on the long side of the triangle), measure the long side of the triangle and add $1\frac{1}{2}$" to this measurement for seam allowances. Cut a square this size, then cut it twice diagonally to make 4 quarter-square triangles.

Quarter-Square Triangles

$1\frac{1}{2}$" + $1\frac{1}{2}$" = 3"

$1\frac{1}{2}$"

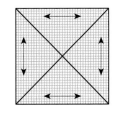

Block size is 4" finished.

One square will provide one triangle for this block plus three other blocks.

CUTTING CALCULATIONS

I hesitate to use a word as intimidating as "calculations" for this heading, but it best fits what I would like to describe about cutting pieces from each fabric in a stash group. Remember, you don't need to worry about having enough yardage of a particular fabric; you just need to have enough pieces of the right color and value. So, what if you do run out of a particular fabric? Cut as many pieces as you can, then choose one of the following options: Cut the remaining pieces from one or more of the other fabrics in the stash group, or add additional fabrics to your group that fit the assigned criteria. Trust me, no one is going to count the number of times you use each fabric. It's the variety of similar-but-different fabrics that makes your quilt special.

To determine how many pieces to cut from each fabric within a particular group, divide the number of pieces needed by the number of fabrics in the group. Sometimes it works out to an even number and sometimes you will need to cut a few additional pieces from some of the fabrics.

For example, suppose you need 160 squares, each 2" × 2", from a stash group of medium red fabrics. Let's say you've grouped 8 fabrics from your stash. If you divide the 160 squares by the 8 fabrics, you discover that you need to cut 20 squares from each red fabric.

To determine how many strips you will need to cut from each of the red fabrics in order to cut those 20 squares, divide the width of the fabric by the width of the cut piece. If you have a full width of fabric, use 40". Therefore, 40" divided by 2" equals 20 squares, which is exactly the number you need. That means you can cut one 2"-wide strip from each of the 8 red fabrics, then cut each of those strips into 2" × 2" squares to get the 160 squares needed.

Suppose you don't have a full width, but a piece that is only 18" wide. Dividing 18" by 2" tells you that you can cut 9 squares from each 2" strip. That means you will need to cut two strips, each 2" wide, from that fabric to get 18 squares. Cut a 2" × 4" strip to get the 2 remaining squares.

The chart at right indicates how many squares can be cut from a 40"-long strip.

Cutting Tips

- If you need several pieces of the same size, layer fabrics and cut multiple pieces at once. If you press the fabrics with an iron as you layer them, they will stick together as you cut.
- Cut all the pieces for the quilt at once, and label them. For traditional piecing, label the pieces with the cut size. For machine paper piecing, label the pieces with the location number. I use small stick-on notes for labeling.
- To simplify cutting for machine paper piecing, cut a size that will accommodate several slightly different patches. For example, in "Play the Sunset" (page 30), the cutting chart calls for 256 black rectangles, each 1½" × 3", for pieces #9, #10, #13, and #14 in block G58 and G59 bottom. Even though #9 and #10 are slightly smaller than #13 and #14, one size will work for all the pieces.

CUTTING SQUARES FROM 40"-LONG STRIPS

Cut Size of Square	No. of Squares
1½"	26
1¾"	22
2"	20
2¼"	17
2½"	16
2¾"	14
3"	13
3¼"	12
3½"	11
3¾"	10
4"	10
4¼"	9
4½"	8
4¾"	8
5"	8
5¼"	7
5½"	7
5¾"	6
6"	6
6¼"	6
6½"	6
6¾"	5
7"	5
7¼"	5
7½"	5
7¾"	5
8"	5

Block Assembly

It is important that you sew with an accurate $\frac{1}{4}$" seam allowance. Sewing with a wider or narrower seam allowance will result in inaccuracies and frustration. Take the time to check your $\frac{1}{4}$" seam by doing the following:

Cut four strips of fabric, each $1\frac{1}{2}$" × 3", and join the long sides. Press. Measure the finished unit to see if it is exactly $4\frac{1}{2}$" wide. If it is, you are ready to sew. If it isn't, you need to create an accurate $\frac{1}{4}$" sewing guide.

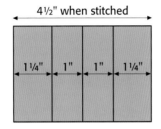

4½" when stitched

1¼" 1" 1" 1¼"

To make a sewing guide, place a rotary ruler under the presser foot and slowly drop the needle until it hits the $\frac{1}{4}$" line. Place several layers of masking tape along the edge of the ruler.

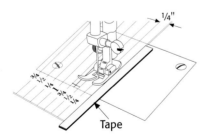

¼"

Tape

If your presser foot overlaps the $\frac{1}{4}$" position and your sewing machine has a movable needle, move the needle to the right and try again. If you do not have this option, cut a notch in the tape under the presser foot so it will not interfere with the feed dogs.

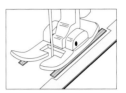

ASSEMBLING TRADITIONALLY PIECED BLOCKS

Arrange the stacks of cut pieces so that you can see all the fabrics for each group you are currently stitching. A cookie sheet or tray comes in handy for this. Whenever possible, chain-sew the pieces together without cutting the thread between them.

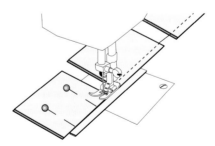

Set the joined units on the ironing board, press them open, and clip the threads. Continue adding pieces, joining units and then rows until the block is complete.

When joining units and rows, machine baste the pieces together first to check for a good match. Set the stitch length to five or six stitches per inch. Baste the beginning, any matching points, and the end. Open the unit to check for a good match. If everything matches, sew the seam again with twelve stitches per inch. If you don't have a good match, simply cut the thread from the bobbin side and remove it. Adjust the pieces as needed and baste again before sewing.

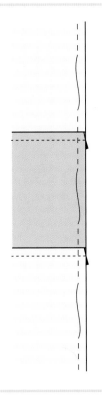

Arrange the blocks in rows to create the quilt top. Move the blocks around a bit until you find a pleasing arrangement. Trust me, you can play with block placements for hours, but a block change here or there really isn't going to make a big impact on the quilt. But you'll sleep better knowing you had that control.

ASSEMBLING PAPER-PIECED BLOCKS

Paper piecing is the perfect way to stitch up intricate designs. If you are new to paper piecing, make one block first to gain experience, then chain-sew subsequent blocks.

Reproducing Paper Foundations

You will need one paper foundation for each of your blocks. The design printed on the foundation is the reverse of the finished block. If you don't have access to a copy machine, trace the design and numbers onto tracing paper using a ruler and a pencil.

If you are using a copy machine, be sure to make all the copies for each quilt project on the same copy machine from the original design. If you want to change the block size, most copy machines have scale options that allow you to enlarge or reduce.

If you would like to use a design from one of my previous paper-piecing books and have a computer and printer, the designs are available on compact disc—the Carol Doak Designer Edition of the Foundation Factory. The designs from this book will be in version 2 on compact disc. See page 112 for purchasing information.

Use lightweight copy paper when reproducing designs on a copy machine or computer printer. Or use Papers for Foundation Piecing. See page 112 for purchasing information. If you use photocopies, cover the pressing surface with a scrap of muslin to protect it from any toner that may transfer from the photocopies.

Paper Piecing

1. Make a copy of the paper foundation for each block you plan to make. Cut out the foundation ½" from the outside solid line.

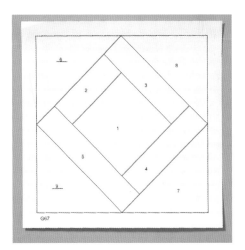

2. Place a size 90/14 needle in the sewing machine and set the stitch length to 18 to 20 stitches per inch. The large needle and short stitch length will make removing the paper easier.
3. Select the foundation and fabric for pieces #1 and #2. Remember to select fabric from each group randomly.

4. Pin piece #1, right side up, on the blank side of the paper over the area marked #1. Make sure it covers the entire area plus a generous seam allowance on all sides.

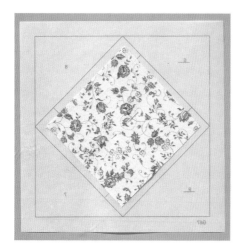

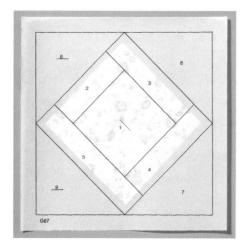

5. Place a postcard, glossy side up, on the line between #1 and #2. Fold the paper across the edge of the postcard to expose excess fabric for patch #1.

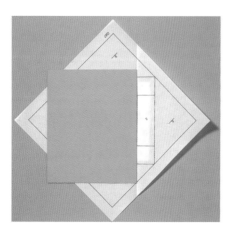

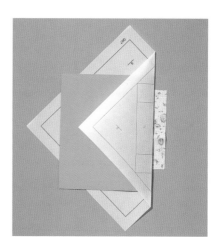

6. Align the ¼" mark on a rotary ruler with the fold and trim the fabric ¼" from the fold. I use the 6" Add-A-Quarter Ruler on the folded edge. The ¼" lip on the edge of the ruler hooks onto the fold and I can trim to ¼" without the ruler moving.

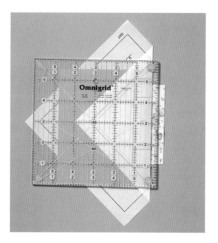

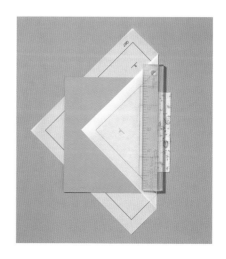

7. Place piece #2 right side up on the blank side of the paper to check for correct placement. Then flip it right sides together with the previous fabric along the just-trimmed edge. Placing the fabric right side up first and looking through the blank side of the paper ensures that the piece is correctly positioned before you sew it. Pin piece #2 in place. You can pin pieces together when you're starting out. As you gain experience, you can just hold the fabric in place.

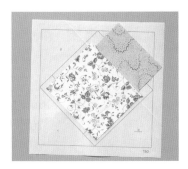

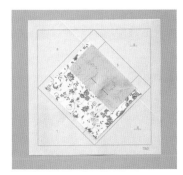

8. Carefully place the foundation, lined side up, under the presser foot and sew on the line between #1 and #2, beginning about ¼" before and ending about ¼" beyond.

9. Clip the threads, open piece #2, and press with a dry iron on a cotton setting. Remember to cover your pressing surface with muslin if you are using photocopies.

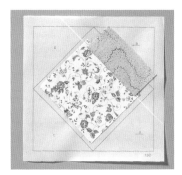

10. Continue in the same manner with pieces #3, #4, and #5, using the following sequence.

   a. Place the postcard on the next line you will sew.
   b. Fold the paper back, exposing the excess fabric. You may need to tear the stitching that extended beyond the seam line away from the foundation. That is okay!
   c. Trim the fabric ¼" from the fold.

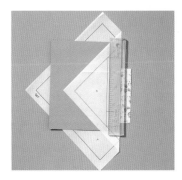

   d. Place the next fabric to be sewn right side up over the area it needs to fill to confirm that it is placed correctly, and then flip it right sides together against the just-trimmed edge.

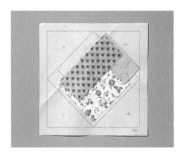

11. When you are ready to add piece #6, place the triangle right side up over the area it needs to fill to position it. Then place the triangle right sides together with the previous piece. To be sure the triangle is centered over the area, align the corner of the triangle on the paper with the corner of the fabric triangle. Stitch, then press the piece open. Continue with the 3 remaining triangles.

12. Align the ¼" line on the rotary ruler with the outside sewing line on the block. Trim the block ¼" from the outside sewing line. Do not remove the paper yet! The paper will stabilize the fabric and provide you with a ¼" line to follow when it's time to join the blocks.

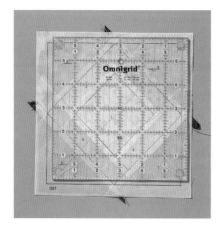

Paper Piecing Tips

◆ If you need to repair a paper foundation, use Scotch Brand Removable tape on the lined side of the paper. Do not touch the iron directly to the tape. This tape is not very sticky and will hold the paper foundation intact until you need to remove it. If you need to take a line of stitching out, place the tape over the stitching before you remove the stitches. The seam can be sewn again without the paper foundation tearing.

◆ Chain-sew similar blocks. Place the blocks on the ironing surface, clip the threads, and press the pieces open. Stack the foundations in the same way so that the previously added pieces can be trimmed ¼" from the next sewing line.

◆ Arrange the stacked pieces for each stash group you are about to stitch so you can see the entire selection. Use the fabrics in sequence as you sew. If the previous fabric in the block is the same as the one you just took from the stack, skip to the next one in the sequence. This way, you'll use the fabrics within each group at the same rate. As you approach the last few pieces, look ahead and assign placements so you won't be left with the same fabrics touching each other in a block.

Quilt Projects

The first eight projects are made with paper piecing methods and the last seven projects are made with traditional machine piecing.

For each quilt, I've indicated how many fabrics were used in each stash group. These are just guidelines—you can increase or decrease the number of fabrics in each group if you want.

The total number of pieces to cut from each stash group is listed in the cutting chart. To determine how many pieces to cut from each fabric, divide the number needed by the number of fabrics in your group. For example, let's say your stash group includes 10 medium blue fabrics and the cutting chart calls for 52 pieces, each 2" × 2". Divide 52 by 10 to find that you need 5 squares from each of your 10 fabrics, plus 2 more squares from 2 of the fabrics.

To make cutting easier, go through the cutting chart for your project and divide the number of pieces for each size by the number of fabrics in your stash group. Use a pencil to mark the resulting number on the chart. This way, you'll be able to see at a glance how many pieces to cut from each fabric.

The number under the "No. of Pieces" heading in the cutting chart indicates the number of squares to cut, which you will sometimes cut in half diagonally once or twice as directed. When you see this symbol (◻) in the cutting list, cut the squares once diagonally to yield two half-square triangles. When you see this symbol (⊠), cut the squares twice diagonally to yield four quarter-square triangles.

There are two materials lists, one for constant fabrics and one for stash fabrics. In the cutting chart, a constant fabric is indicated with this symbol: Ⓒ.

As you look at the materials lists, you'll see the term "similar range," which indicates that fabrics in a group should be close in color, value, and texture. Similar-range groups are generally used for background fabrics.

The block-front drawings included with the paper-pieced quilts show how the block will appear when it is finished. The arrows in the step-by-step illustrations indicate which way to press seam allowances.

Cut border and binding strips from the length of the fabric unless directed otherwise. Bindings are cut as double-fold straight-grain strips. If you prefer to cut bias strips, you will need extra fabric.

PROJECT GAME PLAN

1. Read the front portion of this book.
2. Select a quilt you would like to make.
3. Fill in the block design with your color choices.
4. Gather fabrics for each stash group and select any constant fabrics indicated.
5. Calculate how many pieces to cut from each fabric in each stash group, and write this number directly on the cutting chart. Following the cutting chart, cut the fabric pieces and label them.
6. If you're making a paper-pieced quilt, make the needed paper foundations. The foundations are the reverse of the finished block designs.
7. Make the blocks, chain-stitching pieces whenever possible.
8. Refer to "Assembly and Finishing" on pages 91–96 to assemble the blocks and border(s) and finish the quilt.
9. Most of all, have fun!

PLAY THE SUNSET

By Carol Doak, 1997, Windham, New Hampshire, 60" × 60".
This is the quilt that inspired my passion for stash fabric. A
black background sets off dramatic jewel tones, and gray and
light teal "constants" reinforce the medallion focus.

Information at a Glance:

Finished quilt size: 60" × 60"

Construction method: Paper piecing

Block No.	No. to Make	Finished Size of Unit
G58	20	6" × 6"
G59	44	6" × 6"
G60	8	3" × 3"

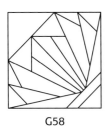 

| G58 | G59 | G60 |

Block-Front Drawings
Full-size patterns are on pages 98–99 and 102.

Materials

CONSTANT FABRICS

■ 2 yds. black for border and binding

□ ½ yd. gray

□ ¼ yd. light teal

3¾ yds. for backing

64" x 64" piece of batting

STASH FABRICS

Use the number of fabrics listed as a general guide—
you can increase or decrease the number of fabrics
as needed. Refer to the cutting chart for blocks
to determine how much fabric you'll need.
See "Quilt Projects" on page 27 for more information.

■ 7 dark purples

■ 7 medium purples

■ 9 fuchsias

■ 6 dark teals

■ 8 medium teals

■ 10 pinks

■ 10 blacks (similar range)

CUTTING FOR SETTING PIECES, BORDERS, AND BINDING

Fabric	No. of Pieces	Dimensions	Location
Black C	6	2" × 40"	Binding*
	1	2" × 10"	Binding*
	4	6½" × 21½"	Side borders*
	4	6½" × 27½"	Top and bottom borders*
	4	3½" × 6½"	Top of G60 blocks

*Cut across the width of the fabric.

CUTTING FOR BLOCKS

Fabric	No. of Pieces	Dimensions	Location Numbers	Block
Dark purples	64	1½" × 6"	1	G58, G59 bottom
Medium purples	64	1½" × 6"	2	G58, G59 bottom
	32	2¾" × 2¾" ◩	18	G58, G59 bottom
	52	1¼" × 2"	2	G59 top, G60
Fuchsias	128	1¼" × 5"	3, 4	G58, G59 bottom
Dark teals	128	1¾" × 6"	7, 8	G58, G59 bottom
	64	1¼" × 5"	17	G58, G59 bottom
	104	1" × 2"	5, 6	G59 top, G60
Medium teals	128	1½" × 5"	11, 12	G58, G59 bottom
	26	2¼" × 2¼" ◩	9	G59 top, G60
Pinks	128	1¾" × 6"	15, 16	G58, G59 bottom
	52	1¼" × 2"	1	G59 top, G60
Gray C	44	3½" × 3½" ◩	5, 6	G59 bottom
Light teal C	52	1" × 5"	10	G59 top, G60
Blacks	20	3½" × 3½" ◩	5, 6	G58
	256	1½" × 3"	9, 10, 13, 14	G58, G59 bottom
	14	4¼" × 4¼" ◩	19	G58
			11	G60
	104	2" × 2" ◩	3, 4, 7, 8	G59 top, G60

Directions

1. Make 20 copies of G58, 44 copies of G59, and 8 copies of G60 (pages 98–99 and 102). Cut out the patterns ½" beyond the outside lines.

2. Make the blocks, placing fabrics as shown.

G58	G59	G60
Make 20.	Make 44.	Make 8.

3. Arrange the G58 and G59 blocks as shown. Sew the blocks into horizontal rows, then join the rows.

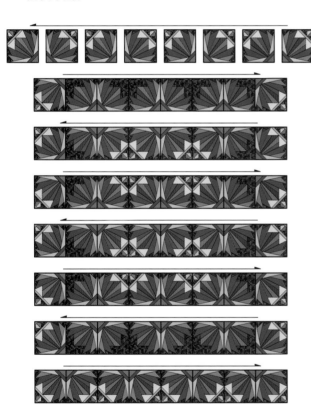

4. Join the G60 blocks in pairs.

Make 4.

5. Sew a 3½" × 6½" black rectangle to each of the units made in step 4.

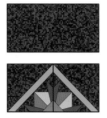 

Make 4.

6. Sew a 6½" × 21½" black strip to each side of a unit made in step 5 for side borders. Make 2. Sew a 6½" × 27½" black strip to each side of the remaining units from step 5 for the top and bottom borders.

7. Sew the borders to the sides of the quilt top, then to the top and bottom.

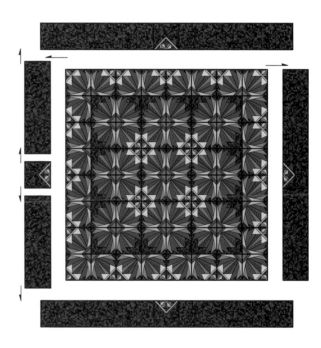

8. Referring to "Assembly and Finishing" on pages 91–96, layer your quilt top with batting and backing; baste. Quilt as desired, bind the edges, and make a label for your quilt.

RED AND GREEN ELEGANCE

By Carol Doak, 1998, Windham, New Hampshire, 51" × 51", quilted by Ellen Peters. Red and green sparkle in this quilt, but a different pair of complementary colors would be equally dramatic. The alternating open areas provide opportunity for lavish quilting.

Information at a Glance

Finished quilt size: 51" × 51"
Construction method: Paper piecing

Block No.	No. to Make	Finished Size of Unit
G61	20	6" × 6"
G62	16	6" × 6"

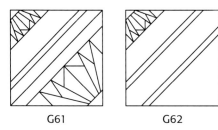

Block-Front Drawings
Full-size patterns are on pages 100–01.

Materials

CONSTANT FABRICS

■ 1¾ yds. dark green for blocks, outer border, and binding

■ ⅞ yd. dark red for blocks and inner border

■ ¾ yd. medium green

3⅛ yds. for backing

55" x 55" piece of batting

STASH FABRICS

Use the number of fabrics listed as a general guide—you can increase or decrease the number of fabrics as needed. Refer to the cutting chart for blocks to determine how much fabric you'll need.
See "Quilt Projects" on page 27 for more information.

□ 10 beiges (similar range)

■ 10 reds

CUTTING FOR BORDERS AND BINDING

Fabric	No. of Pieces	Dimensions	Location
Dark green C	4	2" × 54"	Binding
	2	6½" × 51½"	Top & bottom outer borders
	2	6½" × 39½"	Side outer borders
Dark red C	2	2" × 39½"	Top & bottom inner borders*
	2	2" × 36½"	Side inner borders*

*Cut across the width of the fabric.

CUTTING FOR BLOCKS

Fabric	No. of Pieces	Dimensions	Location Numbers	Block
Dark green C	20	1½" × 10"	14	G61 bottom
Dark red C	52	1" × 9"	15	G61 top
			15, 17	G62
Medium green C	20	1½" × 10"	16	G61 top
	16	2¼" × 10"	16	G62
Beiges	36	2" × 8"	14	G61 top, G62
	8	5¾" × 5¾" ◻	18	G62
	216	1½" × 1½"	3, 4, 7, 8, 11, 12	G61 top, G62
	120	2" × 2"	3, 4, 7, 8, 11, 12	G61 bottom
Reds	252	1" × 2"	1, 2, 5, 6, 9, 10,	G61 top, G62
			13	G61 top, G62
	120	1½" × 4"	1, 2, 5, 6, 9, 10	G61 bottom
	10	2¼" × 2¼" ◻	13	G61 bottom

Directions

1. Make 20 copies of G61 and 16 copies of G62 (pages 100–101). Cut out the patterns ½" beyond the outside lines.

2. Make the blocks, placing fabrics as shown. Do not press the center seam allowance of G61.

G61
Make 20.

G62
Make 16.

3. Arrange the blocks as shown. Where two G61 blocks join, press the center seam allowances in opposite directions. Sew the blocks into horizontal rows, then join the rows.

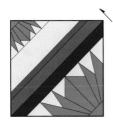 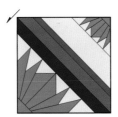

Press center seam allowances
in opposite directions
before joining blocks.

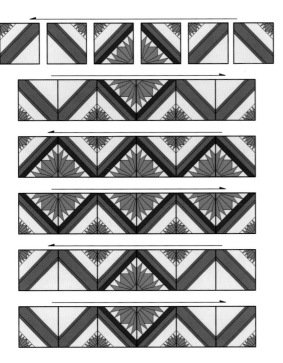

4. Sew the inner border strips to the sides of the quilt top, then to the top and bottom. Repeat for the outer border strips.

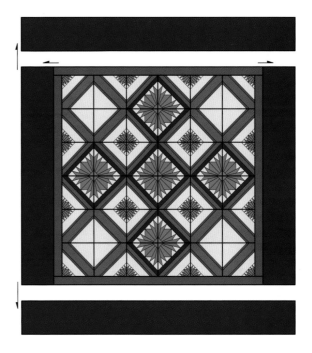

5. Referring to "Assembly and Finishing" on pages 91–96, layer your quilt top with batting and backing; baste. Quilt as desired, bind the edges, and make a label for your quilt.

SAPPHIRE NIGHTS

By Carol Doak, 1998, Windham, New Hampshire, $62\frac{1}{2}$" × $62\frac{1}{2}$", quilted by Judith E. Allen. Since blue is my favorite color, I have lots of blue in my stash. I designed this quilt just so I could use some of my older blue fabrics. To liven things up, I added a bit of fuchsia. At first glance, the blocks in this quilt appear to run diagonally, but they're actually set in straight rows.

Information at a Glance
Finished quilt size: 62½" × 62½"
Construction method: Paper piecing

Block No.	No. to Make	Finished Size of Unit
G63	52	5" × 5"
G64	48	5" × 5"

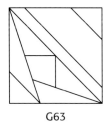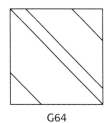

G63   G64

Block-Front Drawings
Full-size patterns are on pages 102–03.

Materials

CONSTANT FABRICS

2 yds. large-scale medium blue print for outer border and binding

1⅝ yds. light blue print for inner border

4 yds. for backing

67" x 67" piece of batting

STASH FABRICS
Use the number of fabrics listed as a general guide—you can increase or decrease the number of fabrics as needed. Refer to the cutting chart for blocks to determine how much fabric you'll need. See "Quilt Projects" on page 27 for more information.

8 navy blues (similar range)

7 fuchsias

8 medium-dark blues

8 medium blues

8 light blues

CUTTING FOR BORDERS AND BINDING

Fabric	No. of Pieces	Dimensions	Location
Medium blue print [C]	4	2" × 66"	Binding
	2	5½" × 53"	Side outer borders
	2	5½" × 63"	Top & bottom outer borders
Light blue print [C]	2	1¾" × 50½"	Side inner borders
	2	1¾" × 53"	Top & bottom inner borders

CUTTING FOR BLOCKS

Fabric	No. of Pieces	Dimensions	Location Numbers	Block
Navy blues	100	2½" × 7"	8	G63
			3	G64
	104	3½" × 3½"	2, 3	G63
Fuchsias	50	3" × 3" ◻	9	G63
			4	G64
	52	1½" × 6"	5	G63
Medium dark blues	48	3" × 8"	1	G64
Medium blues	100	1¼" × 8"	7	G63
			2	G64
	52	1½" × 5"	4	G63
Light blues	50	3" × 3" ◻	6	G63
			5	G64
	52	2½" × 2½"	1	G63

Directions

1. Make 52 copies of G63 and 48 copies of G64 (pages 102–03). Cut out the patterns 1/2" beyond the outside lines.

2. Make the blocks, placing fabrics as shown.

G63
Make 52.

G64
Make 48.

3. Arrange the blocks as shown. Sew the blocks into horizontal rows, then join the rows.

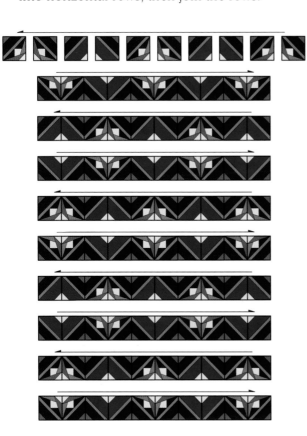

4. Sew the inner border strips to the sides of the quilt top, then to the top and bottom. Repeat for the outer border strips.

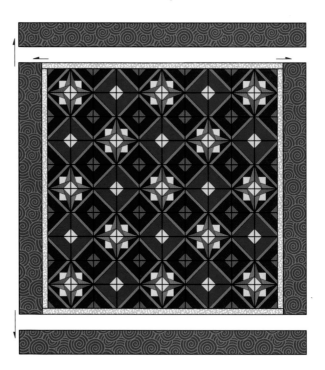

5. Referring to "Assembly and Finishing" on pages 91–96, layer your quilt top with batting and backing; baste. Quilt as desired, bind the edges, and make a label for your quilt.

SPRING'S BOUNTY

By Carol Doak, 1998, Windham, New Hampshire, 66½" ×
66½". Flower-filled baskets bloom in this simple alternating
block quilt. I chose pink for my flowers, but you could use
your favorite color or a variety of different colors.

Information at a Glance

Finished quilt size: $66\frac{1}{2} \times 66\frac{1}{2}$"
Construction method: Paper piecing

Block No.	No. to Make	Finished Size of Unit
B15	17	7" × 7"
G65	12	7" × 7"

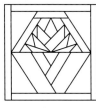

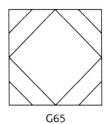

B15   G65

Block-Front Drawings
Full-size patterns are on pages 104–05.

Materials

CONSTANT FABRICS

$2\frac{1}{8}$ yds. dark green for outer border and binding

$1\frac{3}{4}$ yds. medium pink for middle border

1 yd. floral print for inner border

$\frac{1}{8}$ yd. medium gold for flower centers (B15 top)

$4\frac{1}{8}$ yds. for backing

71" x 71" piece of batting

STASH FABRICS

Use the number of fabrics listed as a general guide—you can increase or decrease the number of fabrics as needed. Refer to the cutting chart for blocks to determine how much fabric you'll need. See "Quilt Projects" on page 27 for more information.

8 whites (similar range)

8 medium browns

6 light browns

10 medium dark greens

8 medium light pinks

CUTTING FOR BORDERS AND BINDING

Fabric	No. of Pieces	Dimensions	Location
Dark green C	4	2" × 70"	Binding
	2	7½" × 53"	Side outer borders
	2	7½" × 67"	Top & bottom outer borders
Pink C	2	2¼" × 49½"	Side middle borders
	2	2¼" × 53"	Top & bottom middle borders
Floral print	4	7½" × 35½"	Inner borders*

*Cut across the width of the fabric.

CUTTING FOR BLOCKS

Fabric	No. of Pieces	Dimensions	Location Numbers	Block
Medium gold C	17	2" × 2"	1	B15 top
Whites	136	1¼" × 2"	2, 3, 6, 7, 10, 11	B15 top
			14, 15	B15 top
	68	2½" × 5"	19, 20	B15 top
			6, 7	B15 bottom
	68	1¼" × 8"	21	B15 top
			8	B15 bottom
			22, 23	B15
	12	6" × 6"	1	G65
Medium browns	51	1¼" × 4½"	16–18	B15 top
	34	2" × 5½"	4, 5	B15 bottom
Light browns	17	2" × 2"	1	B15 bottom
	34	1½" × 4"	2, 3	B15 bottom
Medium dark greens	68	1" × 3"	8, 9, 12, 13	B15 top
	48	2" × 6½"	2–5	G65
Pinks	34	1½" × 3"	4, 5	B15 top
	24	3" × 3" ◻	6–9	G65

Directions

1. Make 17 copies of B15 and 12 copies of G65 (pages 104–05). Cut out the patterns ¹/₂" beyond the outside lines.

2. Make the blocks, placing fabrics as shown. For B15, trim pieces #6–#8 in the bottom half and #19–#21 in the top half ¹/₄" from the next seam line before joining the halves. Add pieces #22 and #23 to the block after joining the halves.

Add the last 2 pieces after joining halves.

B15
Make 17.

G65
Make 12.

3. Arrange blocks as shown; you'll have 4 B15 blocks left over for the border. Sew the blocks into horizontal rows, then join the rows.

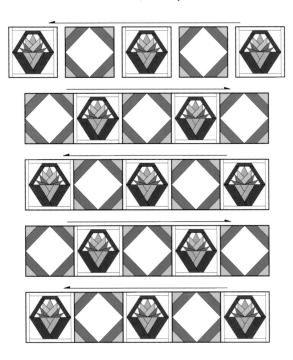

4. Sew the inner border strips to the sides of the quilt top. Sew a B15 block to each end of the remaining inner border strips, then sew the borders to the top and bottom edges of the quilt top.

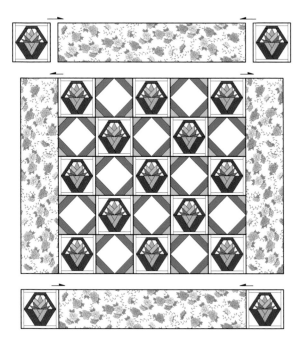

5. Sew the middle border strips to the sides of the quilt top, then to the top and bottom. Repeat for the outer border strips.

6. Referring to "Assembly and Finishing" on pages 91–96, layer your quilt top with batting and backing; baste. Quilt as desired, bind the edges, and make a label for your quilt.

JEWELED FLOWERS

By Carol Doak, 1998, Windham, New Hampshire, 60" × 60",
quilted by Ellen Peters. Just two simple blocks make a dramatic statement. If jewel tones don't suit your mood, make a
quilt for spring in pastels or one for the holidays in red and
green.

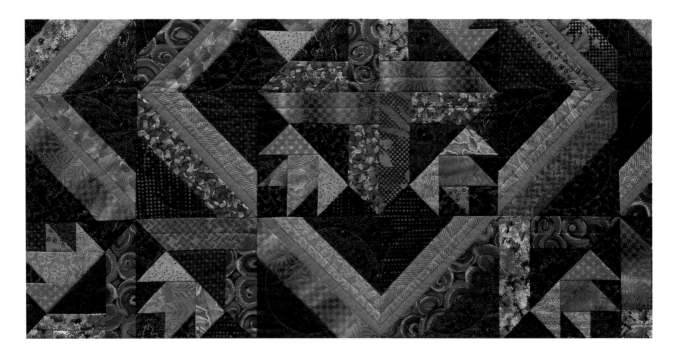

Information at a Glance

Finished quilt size: 60" × 60"
Construction method: Paper piecing

Block No.	No. to Make	Finished Size of Unit
F77	24	6" × 6"
G66	24	6" × 6"

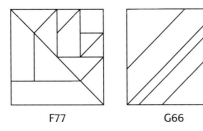

F77   G66

Block-Front Drawings
Full-size patterns are on pages 106–07.

Materials

CONSTANT FABRICS

■ 1¾ yds. black for outer border and binding

■ ⅞ yd. purple for inner border

■ ⅓ yd. pink for G66

3¾ yds. for backing

64" x 64" piece of batting

STASH FABRICS

Use the number of fabrics listed as a general guide—
you can increase or decrease the number of fabrics
as needed. Refer to the cutting chart for blocks
to determine how much fabric you'll need.
See "Quilt Projects" on page 27 for more information.

■ 8 blacks (similar range)

■ 6 medium purples

■ 4 medium teals

■ 6 dark teals

CUTTING FOR BORDERS AND BINDING

Fabric	No. of Pieces	Dimensions	Location
Black [C]	6	2" × 40"	Binding*
	1	2" × 12"	Binding*
	4	6½" × 18½"	Side outer borders*
	4	6½" × 24½"	Top & bottom outer borders*
Purple [C]	4	6½" × 36½"	Inner borders*

**Cut across the width of the fabric.*

CUTTING FOR BLOCKS

Fabric	No. of Pieces	Dimensions	Location Numbers	Block
Pink [C]	24	1¼" × 9½"	1	G66
Blacks	24	2¼" × 2¼"	1	F77 top
	24	2¾" × 2¾" ⧄	3, 5	F77 top
	12	4½" × 4½" ⊠	8, 9	F77 top
	12	4¼" × 4¼" ⧄	1	F77 bottom
	24	5¼" × 5¼" ⧄	3, 5	G66
Medium purples	12	2¾" × 2¾" ⧄	2	F77 top
	24	2" × 4"	4	F77 top
	24	1¾" × 8½"	2	G66
Medium teals	12	4½" × 4½" ⊠	6, 7	F77 top
Dark teals	24	2¼" × 5½"	2	F77 bottom
	24	2¼" × 7"	3	F77 bottom
	24	2" × 9½"	4	G66

Directions

1. Make 24 copies of F77 and 24 copies of G66 (see pages 106–07.) Cut out the patterns ½" beyond the outside lines.
2. Make the blocks, placing fabrics as shown.

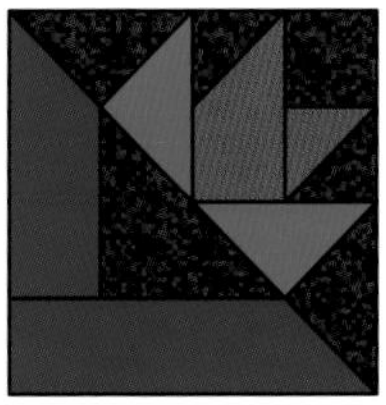

F77
Make 24.

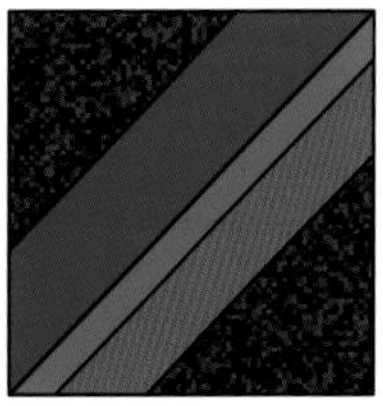

G66
Make 24.

3. Arrange the blocks as shown. Sew the blocks into horizontal rows, then join the rows.

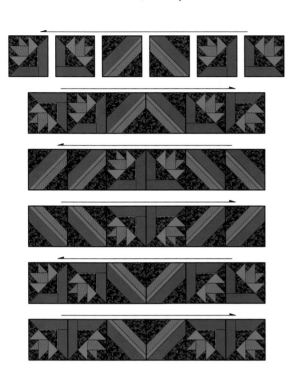

4. Sew the inner border strips to the sides of the quilt top. Sew an F77 block to each end of the remaining border strips, then sew the borders to the top and bottom edges.

5. Sew 2 G66 blocks together. Make 4 units.

 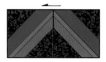

Make 4.

6. To make each side border, sew a $6\frac{1}{2}"\times 18\frac{1}{2}"$ black strip to each side of a unit made in step 5. Sew the borders to the sides of the quilt top. Sew the $6\frac{1}{2}"\times 24\frac{1}{2}"$ black strips to each side of the remaining units made in step 5, and sew these to the top and bottom edges.

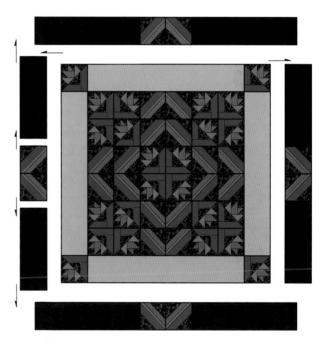

7. The teal fabrics in the border blocks have exposed bias edges. To stabilize them, sew across the teal pieces using a very small stitch, before you remove the paper.

8. Referring to "Assembly and Finishing" on pages 91–96, layer your quilt top with batting and backing; baste. Quilt as desired, bind the edges, and make a label for your quilt.

BLUE AND
YELLOW STASH QUILT

By Carol Doak, 1998, Windham, New Hampshire, 48" × 48",
quilted by Ellen Peters. Blue and yellow look terrific here, but
consider other fabric combinations. A fun motif in the block
square surrounded by colorful strips would make a delightful
baby quilt.

Information at a Glance

Finished quilt size: 48" × 48"

Construction method: Paper piecing

Block No.	No. to Make	Finished Size of Unit
G67	40	6" × 6"

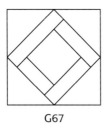

G67

Block-Front Drawing
Full-size pattern is on page 108.

Materials

CONSTANT FABRICS

 1¼ yds. large-scale dark blue/yellow print for border and binding

3 yds. for backing

52" x 52" piece of batting

STASH FABRICS

Use the number of fabrics listed as a general guide—you can increase or decrease the number of fabrics as needed. Refer to the cutting chart for blocks to determine how much fabric you'll need.
See "Quilt Projects" on page 27 for more information.

☐ 6 yellows (similar range)

▨ 6 medium blues

▮ 6 dark blues

☐ 7 light blues

⬚ 7 yellow/blues

CUTTING FOR BORDERS AND BINDING

Fabric	No. of Pieces	Dimensions	Location
Large-scale print ⓒ	5	2" × 40"	Binding*
	4	6½" × 36½"	Borders*

Cut across the width of the fabric.

CUTTING FOR BLOCKS

Fabric	No. of Pieces	Dimensions	Location Numbers	Block
Yellows	40	3¼" × 3¼"	1	G67
Medium blues	80	1½" × 4"	2, 4	G67
Dark blues	80	1½" × 5"	3, 5	G67
Light blues	40	4¼" × 4¼" ◱	8, 9	G67
Yellow/blues	40	4¼" × 4¼" ◱	6, 7	G67

Directions

1. Make 40 copies of G67 (page 108). Cut out the patterns ½" beyond the outside lines.
2. Make the blocks, placing fabrics as shown.

G67
Make 40.

3. Arrange the blocks as shown, rotating them so that colors match at corners. Sew the blocks into horizontal rows, then join the rows.

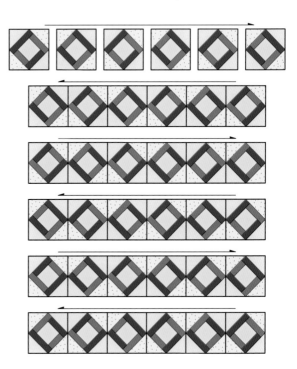

4. Sew the border strips to the sides of the quilt top. Sew a G67 block to each end of the remaining border strips, then sew the borders to the top and bottom edges.

5. Referring to "Assembly and Finishing" on pages 91–96, layer your quilt top with batting and backing; baste. Quilt as desired, bind the edges, and make a label for your quilt.

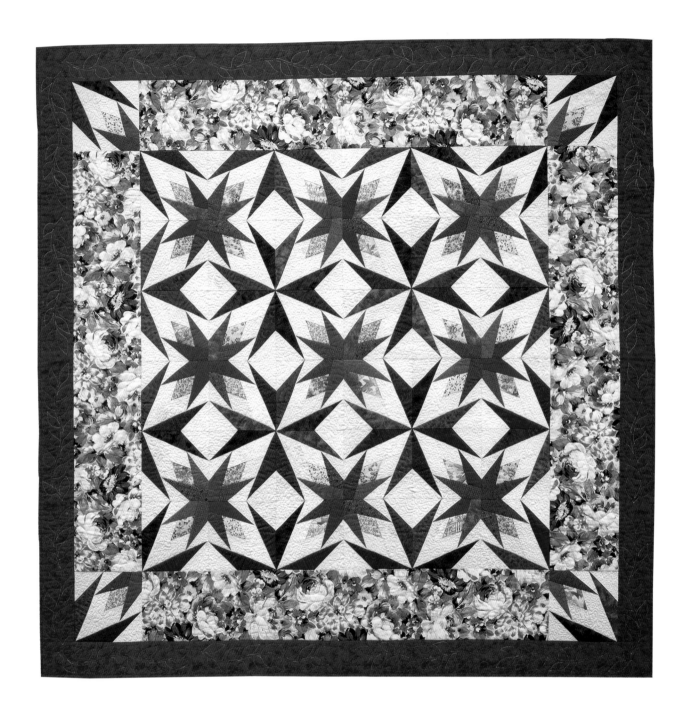

BLUE POSIES

By Carol Doak, 1998, Windham, New Hampshire, 63" × 63", quilted by Ellen Peters. Isn't it amazing how one simple block can produce such a fabulous quilt? I can't wait to make it again using a black background and light flowers.

Information at a Glance

Finished quilt size: 63" × 63"

Construction method: Paper piecing

Block No.	No. to Make	Finished Size of Unit
F78	40	7" × 7"

F78

Block-Front Drawing
Full-size pattern is on page 109.

Materials

CONSTANT FABRICS

2 yds. dark blue for outer border and binding

1 ¼ yds. medium floral print for inner border

4 yds. for backing

67" x 67" piece of batting

STASH FABRICS

Use the number of fabrics listed as a general guide—you can increase or decrease the number of fabrics as needed. Refer to the cutting chart for blocks to determine how much fabric you'll need. See "Quilt Projects" on page 27 for more information.

8 whites (similar range)

8 dark greens

6 medium yellows

8 dark blues

CUTTING FOR BORDERS AND BINDING

Fabric	No. of Pieces	Dimensions	Location
Dark blue Ⓒ	4	2" × 66"	Binding
	2	4" × 56½"	Side outer border
	2	4" × 63½"	Top & bottom outer border
Medium floral print Ⓒ	4	7½" × 42½"	Inner borders*

*You may be able to cut these strips across the width of the fabric;
however, sufficient yardage is provided to cut them from the length.

CUTTING FOR BLOCKS

Fabric	No. of Pieces	Dimensions	Location Numbers	Block
Whites	40	2½" × 4¼"	2	F78
	40	2½" × 7"	3	F78
	80	2" × 5"	6, 7	F78
	40	4¼" × 4¼" ◻	10, 11	F78
Dark greens	80	2¼" × 9"	8, 9	F78
Medium yellows	40	2½" × 4"	1	F78
Dark blues	40	2" × 5½"	4	F78
	40	2" × 6½"	5	F78

Directions

1. Make 40 copies of F78 (see page 109). Cut out the patterns ½" beyond the outside lines.

2. Make the blocks, placing fabrics as shown. Be sure to place the next fabric to be joined right side up over the area it needs to fill before flipping it right sides together with the previous fabric(s). The sewing lines of this block are often shorter than the area the fabric needs to fill.

F78
Make 40.

3. Arrange the blocks as shown. Sew the blocks into horizontal rows, then join the rows.

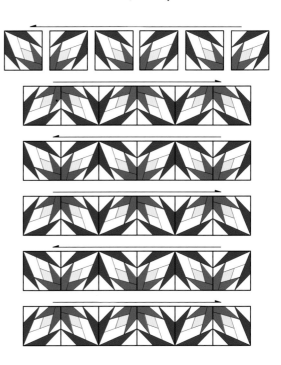

4. Sew the inner border strips to the sides of the quilt top. Add an F78 block to each end of the remaining inner border strips, then sew them to the top and bottom edges.

5. Sew the outer border strips to the sides of the quilt top, then add top and bottom borders.

6. Referring to "Assembly and Finishing" on pages 91–96, layer your quilt top with batting and backing; baste. Quilt as desired, bind the edges, and make a label for your quilt.

VICTORIAN STARS

By Carol Doak, 1998, Windham, New Hampshire, 57" × 57",
quilted by Ellen Peters. I fell in love with the floral print used
in the middle border, and it inspired all the other fabric
choices I made.

Information at a Glance

Finished quilt size: 57" × 57"
Construction method: Paper piecing

Block No.	No. to Make	Finished Size of Unit
G68	24	6" × 6"
G69	16	6" × 6"

 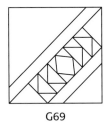

G68   G69

Block-Front Drawings
Full-size patterns are on pages 110–11.

Materials

CONSTANT FABRICS

1¾ yds. black for outer border and binding

1 yd. floral print for middle border

3½ yds. for backing

61" x 61" piece of batting

STASH FABRICS

Use the number of fabrics listed as a general guide—you can increase or decrease the number of fabrics as needed. Refer to the cutting chart for blocks to determine how much fabric you'll need.
See "Quilt Projects" on page 27 for more information.

6 blacks (similar range)

8 grays (similar range)

8 medium pinks

8 medium teals

6 medium purples

CUTTING FOR BORDERS AND BINDING

Fabric	No. of Pieces	Dimensions	Location
Black C	4	2" × 60"	Binding
	2	5" × 48½"	Side outer border
	2	5" × 57½"	Top & bottom outer border
Floral print C	4	6½" × 36½"	Side middle borders*

*Cut across the width of the fabric.

CUTTING FOR BLOCKS

Fabric	No. of Pieces	Dimensions	Location Numbers	Block
Blacks	32	3" × 4½"	1	G68 top & bottom
	32	2½" × 3½"	3	G68 top & bottom
	4	6¼" × 6¼" ◻	23	G69
	4	3¾" × 3¾" ◻	22	G69
Grays	16	3" × 4½"	1	G68 top & bottom
	16	2½" × 3½"	3	G68 top & bottom
	4	6¼" × 6¼" ◻	23	G69
	4	3¾" × 3¾" ◻	22	G69
	96	2" × 2" ◻	2–5, 7, 8, 10, 11, 14, 15, 17, 18	G69
Pinks	48	2" × 7½"	5	G68 top & bottom
	32	2½" × 2½" ◻	6, 9, 13, 16	G69
Teals	48	1½" × 5"	6	G68 top & bottom
	48	2" × 4"	4	G68 top & bottom
	16	3" × 3" ◻	12, 19	G69
	16	1¼" × 6"	21	G69
	16	1¼" × 9½"	20	G69
Purples	48	1¾" × 3½"	2	G68 top & bottom
	12	2½" × 2½" ◻	7	G68
	16	2" × 2"	1	G69

Directions

1. Make 24 copies of G68 and 16 copies of G69 (pages 110–11). Cut out the patterns ½" beyond the outside lines.

2. Make the blocks, placing fabrics as shown. There are some irregular shapes in the G68 block. Remember to place each fabric piece right side up over the area it needs to fill before stitching it in place.

   Before adding piece #7, trim fabric #6, ¼" from the sewing line between #6 and #7. Then trim the top and bottom sections ¼" beyond the outside line. Join the top and bottom sections, then add piece #7 and trim the fabric even with the edge of the paper.

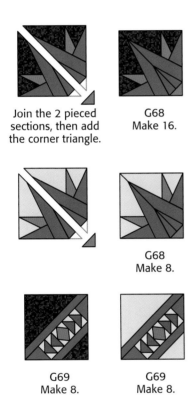

Join the 2 pieced sections, then add the corner triangle.

G68
Make 16.

G68
Make 8.

G69
Make 8.

G69
Make 8.

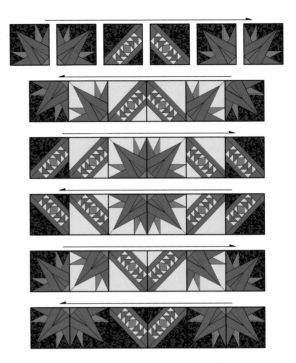

Assembly and Finishing

1. Arrange the blocks as shown above right. Sew the blocks into horizontal rows, then join the rows.

2. Sew the inner border strips to the sides of the quilt top. Add a G68 block to each end of the remaining inner border strips, then sew them to the top and bottom edges.

3. Sew outer border strips to the sides of the quilt top, then to the top and bottom edges.

4. Referring to "Assembly and Finishing" on pages 91–96, layer your quilt top with batting and backing; baste. Quilt as desired, bind the edges, and make a label for your quilt.

FIRE STARS

By Sherry Reis, 1998, Worthington, Ohio, 57" × 57". Warm reds, oranges, and yellows glow against a dark background. This design could easily be worked in a variety of colors. Just choose three colors and a contrasting background, and watch the sparks fly!

Information at a Glance

Finished quilt size: 57" × 57"

Construction method: Traditional piecing

Block	No. to Make	Finished Size of Block
Old Maid's Puzzle	40	6" × 6"

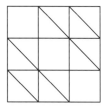

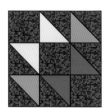

Old Maid's Puzzle Block

Materials

CONSTANT FABRICS

1¾ yds. dark red for outer border and binding

1 yd. black for middle border

3½ yds. for backing

61" x 61" piece of batting

STASH FABRICS

Use the number of fabrics listed as a general guide—you can increase or decrease the number of fabrics as needed. Refer to the cutting chart for blocks to determine how much fabric you'll need. See "Quilt Projects" on page 27 for more information.

10 blacks (similar range)

8 medium oranges

8 medium reds

8 light yellows

CUTTING FOR BORDERS AND BINDING

Fabric	No. of Pieces	Dimensions	Location
Dark red C	4	2" × 60"	Binding
	2	5" × 48½"	Side outer border
	2	5" × 57½"	Top & bottom outer border
Black C	4	6½" × 36½"	Middle border*

*Cut across the width of the fabric.

CUTTING FOR BLOCKS

Fabric	No. of Pieces	Dimensions	
Blacks	120	2½" × 2½"	
	120	2⅞" × 2⅞"	◹
Medium oranges	40	2⅞" × 2⅞"	◹
Medium reds	40	2⅞" × 2⅞"	◹
Light yellows	40	2⅞" × 2⅞"	◹

Directions

1. Sew a black triangle to each of the orange, red, and yellow triangles.

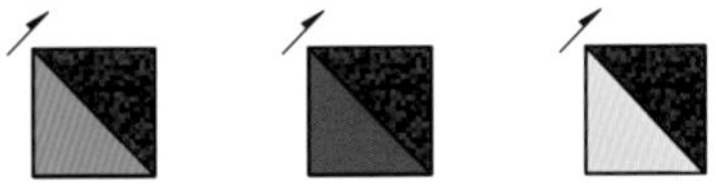

Make 80.   Make 80.   Make 80.

2. Join the triangle units made in step 1 and black squares to make rows.

Make 40.   Make 40.   Make 40.

3. Join the rows to make Old Maid's Puzzle blocks. Make 40 blocks.

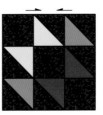

Make 40.

62

Assembly and Finishing

1. Arrange the blocks as shown. Sew the blocks into horizontal rows, then join the rows.

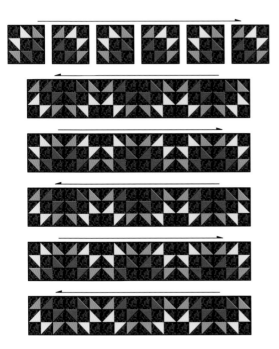

2. Sew the inner border strips to the sides of the quilt top. Sew a patchwork block to each end of the remaining inner border strips, then sew the strips to the top and bottom of the quilt top.

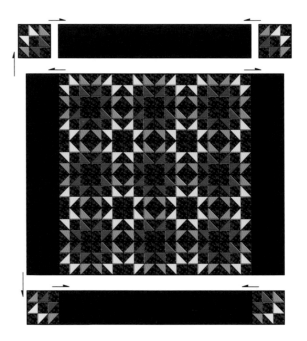

3. Sew outer border strips to the sides of the quilt top, then to the top and bottom edges.

4. Referring to "Assembly and Finishing" on pages 91–96, layer your quilt top with batting and backing; baste. Quilt as desired, bind the edges, and make a label for your quilt.

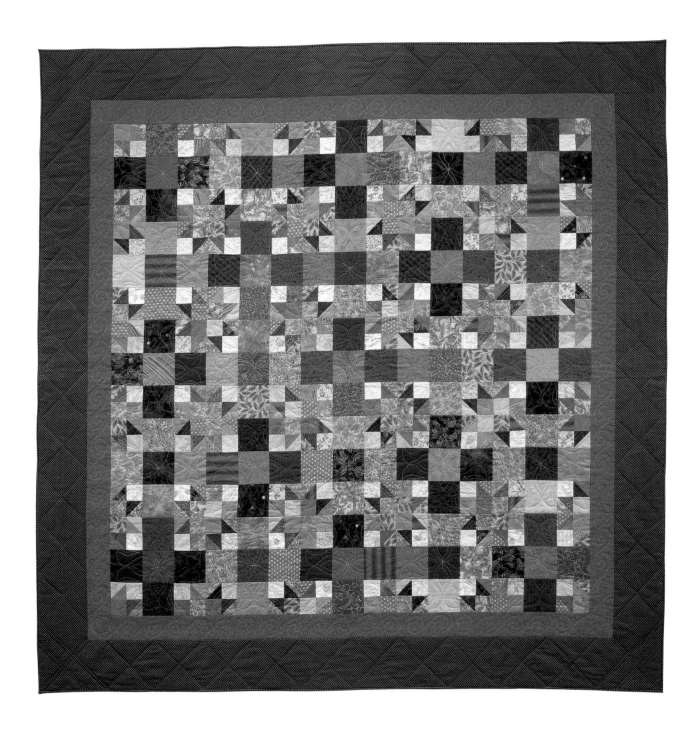

PLUM CRAZY

By Virginia Guaraldi, 1998, Londonderry, New Hampshire, 78" × 78". One simple block made in two colorways yields fabulous results in this quilt. Where the block corners meet, sparkling stars form.

Information at a Glance

Finished quilt size: 78" × 78"
Construction method: Traditional piecing

Block	No. to Make	Finished Size of Block
Star block 1	13	12" × 12"
Star block 2	12	12" × 12"

Materials

CONSTANT FABRICS

2⅜ yds. dark purple
for outer border and binding

2 yds. dark pink for inner border

4¾ yds. for backing

82" x 82" piece of batting

STASH FABRICS

Use the number of fabrics listed as a general guide—
you can increase or decrease the number of fabrics
as needed. Refer to the cutting chart for blocks
to determine how much fabric you'll need.
See "Quilt Projects" on page 27 for more information.

10 light purples

10 medium pinks

10 light pinks

10 medium purples

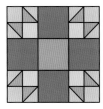

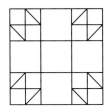

Star Block 1

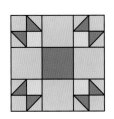

Star Block 2

CUTTING FOR BORDERS AND BINDING

Fabric	No. of Pieces	Dimensions	Location
Dark purple C	4	2" × 81"	Binding
	2	6½" × 66½"	Side outer border
	2	6½" × 78½"	Top & bottom outer border
Dark pink C	2	3½" × 60½"	Side inner border
	2	3½" × 66½"	Top & bottom inner border

CUTTING FOR BLOCKS

Fabric	No. of Pieces	Dimensions	Block
Light purples	48	4½" × 4½"	Star block 2
	100	2½" × 2½"	Star blocks 1 & 2
	100	2⅞" × 2⅞" ◲	Star blocks 1 & 2
Medium pinks	13	4½" × 4½"	Star block 1
	52	2⅞" × 2⅞" ◲	Star block 1
Light pinks	100	2½" × 2½"	Star blocks 1 & 2
Medium purples	64	4½" × 4½"	Star blocks 1 & 2
	48	2⅞" × 2⅞" ◲	Star block 2

Directions

1. Join light purple and medium pink triangles for Star block 1. Join light purple and medium purple triangles for Star block 2.

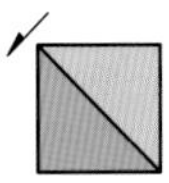

Star Block 1
Make 104.

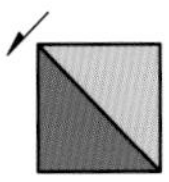

Star Block 2
Make 96.

2. Sew 2½" light pink and light purple squares to the units made in step 1.

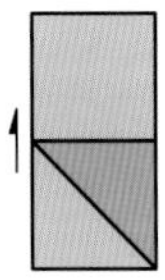

Star Block 1
Make 52.

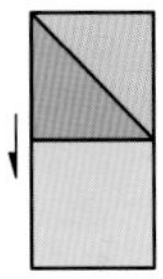

Star Block 1
Make 52.

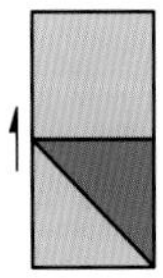

Star Block 2
Make 48.

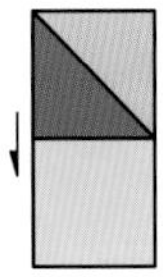

Star Block 2
Make 48.

3. Sew the units for Star block 1 together; repeat with the Star block 2 units.

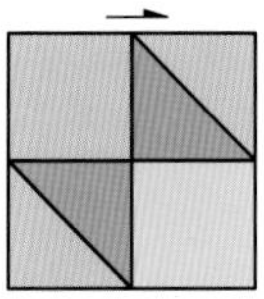

Star Block 1
Make 52.

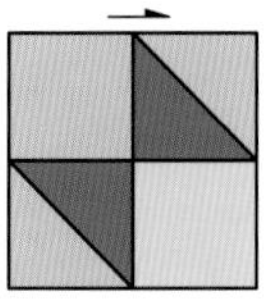

Star Block 2
Make 48.

4. Sew the Star block 1 units to opposite sides of medium purple squares. Sew Star block 2 units to opposite sides of light purple squares.

 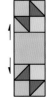

Star Block 1
Make 26.

Star Block 2
Make 24.

5. For Star block 1, join medium pink and medium purple squares. For Star block 2, join light and medium purple squares.

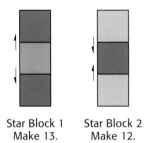

Star Block 1
Make 13.

Star Block 2
Make 12.

6. Join the rows to make Star blocks 1 and 2.

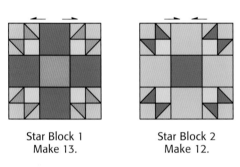

Star Block 1
Make 13.

Star Block 2
Make 12.

Assembly and Finishing

1. Arrange the blocks as shown. Sew the blocks into horizontal rows, then join the rows.

2. Sew the side inner border strips to the quilt top, then add the top and bottom borders. Repeat for the outer border strips.

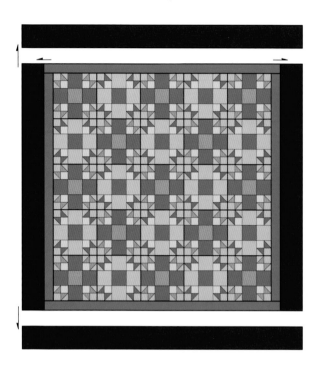

3. Referring to "Assembly and Finishing" on pages 91–96, layer your quilt top with batting and backing; baste. Quilt as desired, bind the edges, and make a label for your quilt.

STAR MEDALLION

By Helen Weinman, 1998, Centerville, Massachusetts, 66" × 66". These blocks are wonderfully versatile—in the middle of the quilt, they form stars; along the outer edges, they form an intricate pieced border. Stitch this up in blue and white, and you can't go wrong.

Information at a Glance

Finished quilt size: 66" × 66"
Construction method: Traditional piecing

Block	No. to Make	Finished Size of Block
Scrap block 1	28	6" × 6"
Scrap block 2	36	6" × 6"

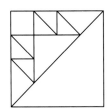

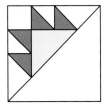
Scrap Block 1

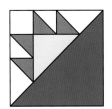
Scrap Block 2

Materials

CONSTANT FABRICS

2⅛ yds. navy for outer border and binding

1¾ yds. light blue for inner border

4 yds. for backing

70" x 70" piece of batting

STASH FABRICS

Use the number of fabrics listed as a general guide—
you can increase or decrease the number of fabrics
as needed. Refer to the cutting chart for blocks
to determine how much fabric you'll need.
See "Quilt Projects" on page 27 for more information.

10 whites (similar range)

10 light blues

10 medium blues

10 dark blues

CUTTING FOR BORDERS AND BINDING

Fabric	No. of Pieces	Dimensions	Location
Navy ©C	4	2" × 70"	Binding
	2	6½" × 54½"	Side outer border
	2	6½" × 66½"	Top & bottom outer border
Light blue ©C	2	3½" × 48½"	Side inner border
	2	3½" × 54½"	Top & bottom inner border

CUTTING FOR BLOCKS

Fabric	No. of Pieces	Dimensions	Block
Whites	14	6⅞" × 6⅞" ◹	Scrap block 1
	64	2" × 2"	Scrap block 1 & 2
	64	2⅜" × 2⅜" ◹	Scrap block 1 & 2
	32	4¼" × 4¼" ◻	Scrap block 1 & 2
Light blues	32	3⅞" × 3⅞" ◹	Scrap block 1 & 2
Medium blues	128	2⅜" × 2⅜" ◹	Scrap block 1 & 2
Dark blues	18	6⅞" × 6⅞" ◹	Scrap block 2

Directions

1. Sew each 2⅜" white triangle to a medium blue triangle.

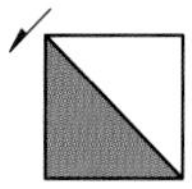

Make 128.

2. Sew the remaining medium blue triangles to the 4¼" white triangles to make units A and B.

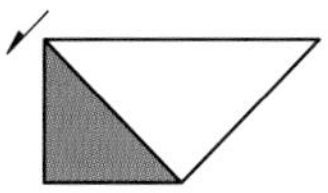

Unit A
Make 64.

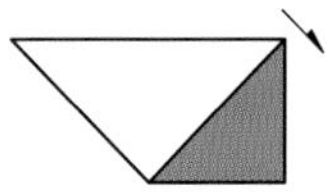

Unit B
Make 64.

3. Sew the units made in step 1 to the units made in step 2. Keep the A and B units in separate stacks.

Unit A
Make 64.

Unit B
Make 64.

4. Sew a light blue triangle to each A unit made in step 3.

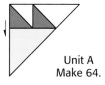

Unit A
Make 64.

5. Sew a white square to each B unit made in step 3.

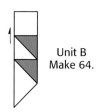

Unit B
Make 64.

6. Join the units made in steps 4 and 5.

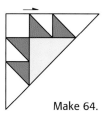

Make 64.

7. Sew a 6⅞" white triangle to 28 of the units made in step 6 to make Scrap block 1. Sew the 6⅞" dark blue triangles to the 36 remaining units to make Scrap block 2.

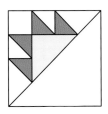 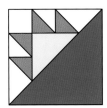

Scrap Block 1
Make 28.

Scrap Block 2
Make 36.

Press seam allowances toward large triangle
except when joining blocks as shown;
then press seam allowances in opposite directions.

Assembly and Finishing

1. Arrange the blocks as shown. Sew the blocks into horizontal rows, then join the rows.

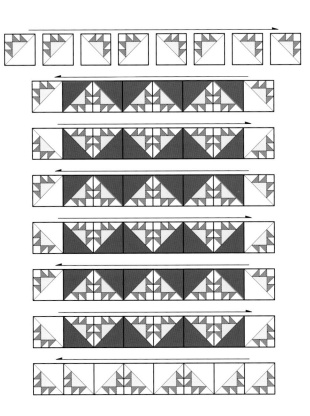

2. Sew the side inner border strips to the quilt top, then add the top and bottom borders. Repeat for the outer border strips.

3. Referring to "Assembly and Finishing" on pages 91–96, layer your quilt top with batting and backing; baste. Quilt as desired, bind the edges, and make a label for your quilt.

SOFT SCRAP QUILT

By Ursula Reikes, 1998, Ivins, Utah, 66" × 66". Go bold and bright or soft and sweet like the pastel quilt shown here. This geometric design lends itself to a variety of interpretations.

Information at a Glance

Finished quilt size: 66" × 66"
Construction method: Traditional piecing

Block	No. to Make	Finished Size of Block
Split Nine Patch	36	9" × 9"

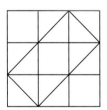

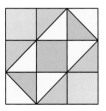

Split Nine Patch

Materials

CONSTANT FABRICS

2⅛ yds. medium blue
for outer border and binding

4⅛ yds. for backing

70" x 70" piece of batting

STASH FABRICS

Use the number of fabrics listed as a general guide—
you can increase or decrease the number of fabrics
as needed. Refer to the cutting chart for blocks
to determine how much fabric you'll need.
See "Quilt Projects" on page 27 for more information.

9 yellows

9 medium pinks

9 light greens

9 light blues

CUTTING FOR BORDERS AND BINDING

Fabric	No. of Pieces	Dimensions	Location
Medium blue C	4	2" × 70"	Binding
	2	6½" × 54½"	Side outer borders
	2	6½" × 66½"	Top & bottom outer borders

CUTTING FOR BLOCKS

Fabric	No. of Pieces	Dimensions
Yellows	108	3⅞" × 3⅞" ◹
Medium pinks	72	3⅞" × 3⅞" ◹
Light greens	36	3½" × 3½"
	36	3⅞" × 3⅞" ◹
Light blues	72	3½" × 3½"

Directions

1. Sew a yellow triangle to each pink triangle.

Make 144.

2. Sew the remaining yellow triangles to each green triangle.

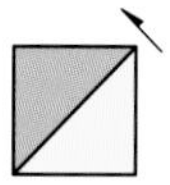

Make 72.

3. Join units from steps 1 and 2 with blue squares. Press the seam allowances up in 36 units and down in 36 units.

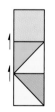

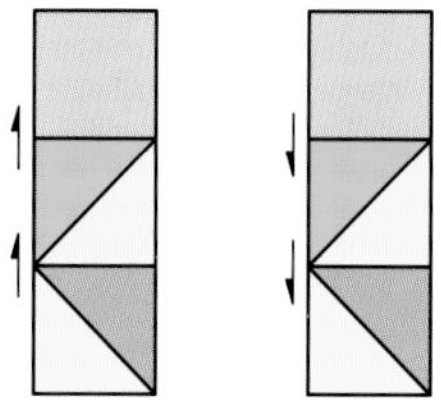

Make 72.
Press seam allowances up for 36 units and down for 36 units.

4. Sew 2 pink units to each green square.

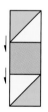

Make 36.

5. Join the rows to make the block.

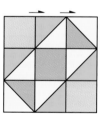

Make 36.

Assembly and Finishing

1. Arrange the blocks as shown. Sew the blocks into horizontal rows, then join the rows.

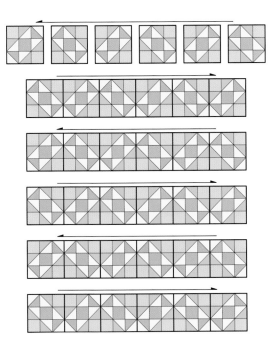

2. Sew outer border strips to the sides of the quilt top, then to the top and bottom edges.

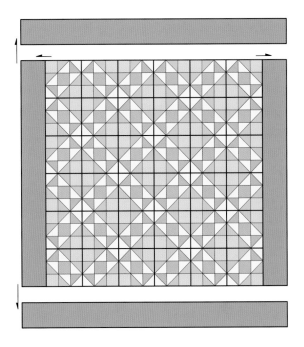

3. Referring to "Assembly and Finishing" on pages 91–96, layer your quilt top with batting and backing; baste. Quilt as desired, bind the edges, and make a label for your quilt.

HOMETOWN

By Ellen Peters, 1998, Laconia, New Hampshire, 80" × 80".
Ellen featured wonderful seasonal quilt designs in the outer
pieced border. She machine quilted sunbursts across the top,
flowers on the right, snowflakes across the bottom and leaves
on the left.

Information at a Glance

Finished quilt size: 80" × 80"
Construction method: Traditional piecing

Block	No. to Make	Finished Size of Block
Tree Block	16	8" × 8"
House Block	16	8" × 8"
Geometric Block	32	8" × 8"

Tree Block   House Block   Geometric Block

Materials

CONSTANT FABRICS

2⅓ yds. dark green
for outer border and binding

5 yds. for backing

84" x 84" piece of batting

STASH FABRICS

Use the number of fabrics listed as a general guide—
you can increase or decrease the number of fabrics
as needed. Refer to the cutting chart for blocks
to determine how much fabric you'll need.
See "Quilt Projects" on page 27 for more information.

10 blacks

10 light blues (similar range)

10 medium greens

5 beiges

10 dark reds

10 dark blues

CUTTING FOR BORDERS AND BINDING

Fabric	No. of Pieces	Dimensions	Location
Dark green Ⓒ	4	2" × 83"	Binding
	2	6½" × 68½"	Side outer borders
	2	6½" × 80½"	Top & bottom outer borders
Blacks	28	2½" × 8½"	Inner borders*
	4	2½" × 10½"	Inner borders*

See step 2 on page 80 for piecing inner borders.

CUTTING FOR BLOCKS

Fabric	No. of Pieces	Dimensions	Block
Blacks	4	7¼" × 7¼" ⊠	House
	16	1½" × 3½"	House
	16	1½" × 1½"	Tree
Light blues	16	9¼" × 9¼" ⊠	Geometric
	32	3⅞" × 3⅞" ◩	Tree & house
	32	2⅞" × 2⅞" ◩	Tree
	64	1½" × 7½"	Tree & house
	32	1½" × 4½"	Tree
	32	1½" × 4"	Tree
Medium greens	16	1½" × 8½"	House
	4	7¼" × 7¼" ⊠	Tree
	8	5¼" × 5¼" ⊠	Tree
Beiges	32	2" × 2"	House
Dark reds	16	1½" × 6½"	House
	64	1" × 3½"	House
	32	2" × 2"	House
Dark blues	16	9¼" × 9¼" ⊠	Geometric

Tree Blocks

1. Sew two 3⅞" light blue triangles to each of the 7¼" medium green triangles.

Make 16.

2. Sew two 2⅞" light blue triangles to each of the 5¼" medium green triangles.

Make 32.

3. Join 2 units made in step 2. Add a 1½" × 4½" light blue rectangle to each side.

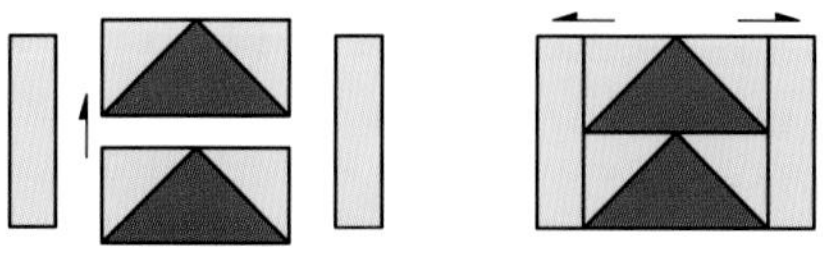

4. Join the units made in steps 1 and 3. Add a 1½" × 7½" light blue rectangle to each side.

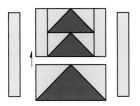

Make 16.

5. Sew two 1½" × 4" light blue rectangles to each of the 1½" black squares.

Make 16.

6. Join the units made in steps 4 and 5 to complete the block.

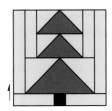

Make 16.

House Blocks

1. Sew the 2" beige squares to the 2" red squares. Add a 1" × 3½" red rectangle to each side.

Make 32.

2. Sew 2 units made in step 1 to a 1½" × 3½" black rectangle. Add a 1½" × 6½" red rectangle to the top of the unit.

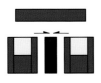

Make 16.

3. Sew two 3⅞" light blue triangles to each of the 7¼" black triangles.

Make 16.

4. Join the units made in steps 2 and 3. Sew a 1½" × 7½" light blue rectangle to each side, and a 1½" × 8½" medium green rectangle to the bottom to complete the block.

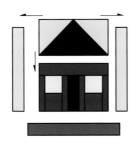

Make 16.

Geometric Blocks

Join the large light blue and dark blue triangles to make blocks.

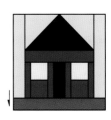

Make 32.

Assembly and Finishing

1. Arrange the blocks as shown. Sew the blocks into horizontal rows, then join the rows.

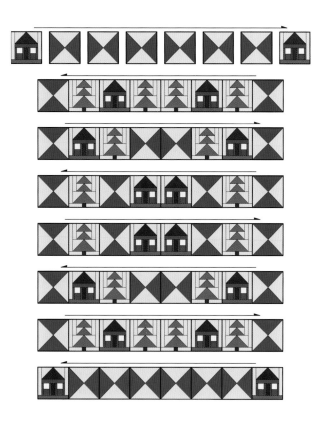

2. Join eight 2½" × 8½" black rectangles to make each of 2 inner side borders. Join 6 rectangles to make each of the top and bottom borders. Add a 2½" × 10½" black rectangle to each end of the top and bottom borders.

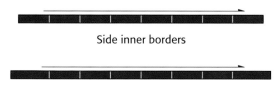

Side inner borders

Top and bottom inner borders

3. Sew the pieced side borders to the quilt top, then add the top and bottom borders. Sew the outer borders to the quilt top in the same order.

4. Referring to "Assembly and Finishing" on pages 91–96, layer your quilt top with batting and backing; baste. Quilt as desired, bind the edges, and make a label for your quilt.

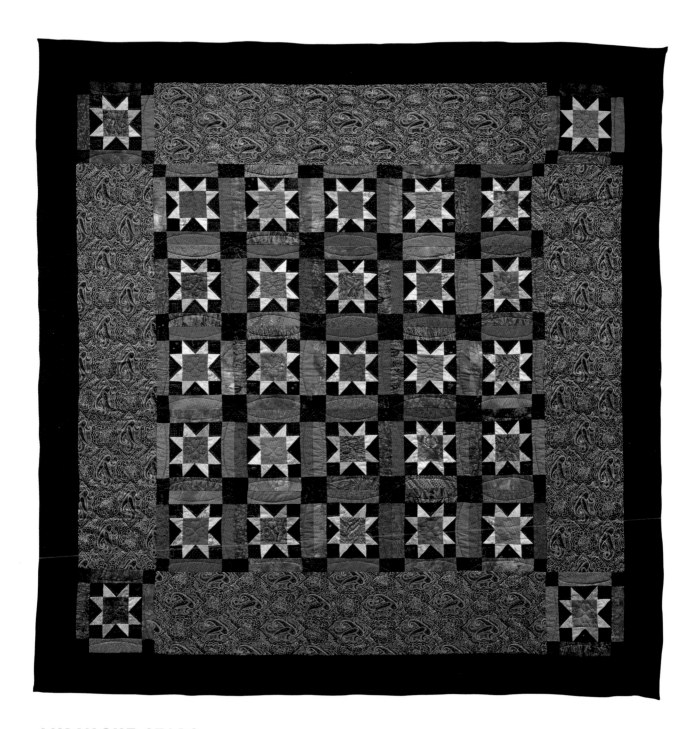

MIDNIGHT STARS

By Pamela Ludwig, 1998, Windham, New Hampshire, 72" × 72". You don't need to piece complicated blocks to make a compelling design. These Star blocks form lively secondary patterns when set side by side.

Information at a Glance

Finished quilt size: 72" × 72"
Construction method: Traditional piecing

Block	No. to Make	Finished Size of Block
Star block 1	16	9" × 9"
Star block 2	13	9" × 9"

Materials

CONSTANT FABRICS

■ 2¼ yds. black for outer border and binding

▨ 1⅜ yds. print for inner border

4½ yds. for backing

76" x 76" piece of batting

STASH FABRICS

Use the number of fabrics listed as a general guide—you can increase or decrease the number of fabrics as needed. Refer to the cutting chart for blocks to determine how much fabric you'll need. See "Quilt Projects" on page 27 for more information.

▨ 10 blacks (similar range)

▨ 10 medium pinks

☐ 10 light pinks

▨ 10 medium teals

☐ 10 light teals

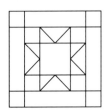

Star Block 1

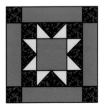

Star Block 2

CUTTING FOR BORDERS AND BINDING

Fabric	No. of Pieces	Dimensions	Location
Black C	4	2" × 75"	Binding
	2	5" × 63½"	Side outer border
	2	5" × 72½"	Top & bottom outer border
Print C	4	9½" × 45½"	Inner border

CUTTING FOR BLOCKS

Fabric	No. of Pieces	Dimensions	Block
Blacks	232	2" × 2"	Star blocks 1 & 2
	29	4¼" × 4¼" ⊠	Star blocks 1 & 2
Medium pinks	52	2" × 6½"	Star block 2
	13	3½" × 3½"	Star block 2
Light pinks	52	2⅜" × 2⅜" ◻	Star block 2
Medium teals	64	2" × 6½"	Star block 1
	16	3½" × 3½"	Star block 1
Light teals	64	2⅜" × 2⅜" ◻	Star block 1

Directions

1. Sew 2 light teal triangles to a black triangle for Star block 1. Sew 2 light pink triangles to a black triangle for Star block 2.

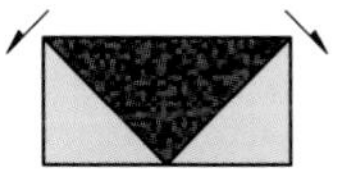

Star Block 1
Make 64.

Star Block 2
Make 52.

2. Sew a black square to each end of *half* the units made in step 1.

Star Block 1
Make 32.

Star Block 2
Make 26.

3. Using the remaining units from step 1, sew 2 light teal units to a medium teal square for Star block 1. Sew 2 light pink units to a medium pink square for Star block 2.

Star Block 1
Make 16.

Star Block 2
Make 13.

4. Join matching units as shown.

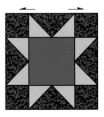

Star Block 1
Make 16.

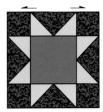

Star Block 2
Make 13.

5. Sew medium teal rectangles to the Star block 1 units. Repeat with medium pink rectangles and Star block 2 units.

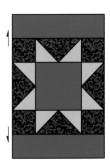

Star Block 1
Make 16.

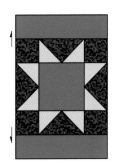

Star Block 2
Make 13.

6. Sew black squares to each end of the remaining medium teal and medium pink rectangles.

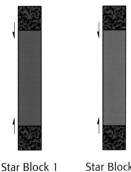

Star Block 1
Make 32.

Star Block 2
Make 26.

7. Join matching units from steps 5 and 6 to complete the blocks.

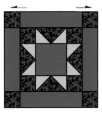

Star Block 1
Make 16.

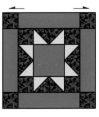

Star Block 2
Make 13.

Assembly and Finishing

1. Arrange the blocks as shown, rotating them as necessary so seam allowances will lock in place. Sew the blocks into horizontal rows, then join the rows.

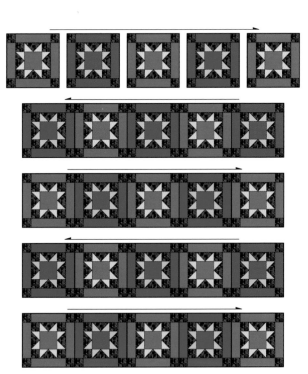

2. Sew the side inner border strips to the quilt top. Sew Star blocks to each end of the remaining inner border strips, then add these to the top and bottom edges.

4. Referring to "Assembly and Finishing" on pages 91–96, layer your quilt top with batting and backing; baste. Quilt as desired, bind the edges, and make a label for your quilt.

3. Sew outer border strips to the sides of the quilt top, then to the top and bottom edges.

NATURE'S GARDEN

By Colleen Pennington, 1998, Columbus, Ohio, 60" × 60".
Colleen used autumn colors for this quilt, but you could use
the palette of any season—or of any time of day. Vivid colors
against a dark background could represent a garden at night.

Information at a Glance

Finished quilt size: 60" × 60"

Construction method: Traditional piecing

Block	No. to Make	Finished Size of Block
Butterfly 1	16	6" × 6"
Butterfly 2	8	6" × 6"
Flower 1	8	6" × 6"
Flower 2	8	6" × 6"

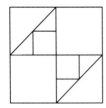 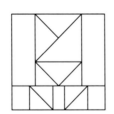

Butterfly Block 1   Butterfly Block 2   Flower Block 1   Flower Block 2

Materials

CONSTANT FABRICS

2 yds. dark green
for outer border and binding

⅞ yd. dark gold for inner border

3¾ yds. for backing

64" x 64" piece of batting

STASH FABRICS

Use the number of fabrics listed as a general guide—
you can increase or decrease the number of fabrics
as needed. Refer to the cutting chart for blocks
to determine how much fabric you'll need.
See "Quilt Projects" on page 27 for more information.

8 beiges (similar range)

8 dark reds

8 medium oranges

8 medium golds

8 yellows

6 medium greens

CUTTING FOR BORDERS AND BINDING

Fabric	No. of Pieces	Dimensions	Location
Dark green C	4	2" × 63"	Binding
	2	6½" × 48½"	Side outer borders
	2	6½" × 60½"	Top & bottom outer borders
Dark gold C	4	6½" × 36½"	Inner borders*

*Cut across the width of the fabric.

CUTTING FOR BLOCKS

Fabric	No. of Pieces	Dimensions	Block
Beiges	32	2" × 5"	Flower blocks 1 & 2
	4	4¼" × 4¼" ⊠	Flower blocks 1 & 2
	32	2⅜" × 2⅜" ◹	Flower blocks 1 & 2
	32	1⅝" × 2"	Flower blocks 1 & 2
	48	3½" × 3½"	Butterfly blocks 1 & 2
	24	3⅞" × 3⅞" ◹	Butterfly blocks 1 & 2
Dark reds	4	3⅞" × 3⅞" ◹	Flower block 1
	32	2" × 2"	Butterfly block 1
Medium oranges	4	4¼" × 4¼" ⊠	Flower block 1
	32	2⅜" × 2⅜" ◹	Butterfly block 1
Medium golds	4	3⅞" × 3⅞" ◹	Flower block 2
	16	2" × 2"	Butterfly block 2
Yellows	4	4¼" × 4¼" ⊠	Flower block 2
	16	2⅜" × 2⅜" ◹	Butterfly block 2
Medium greens	16	2⅜" × 2⅜" ◹	Flower blocks 1 & 2
	16	1¼" × 2"	Flower blocks 1 & 2

Butterfly Blocks

1. Sew two 2⅜" orange triangles to each of the 2" red squares; add a 3⅞" beige triangle. Sew two 2⅜" yellow triangles to each of the 2" gold squares; add a 3⅞" beige triangle.

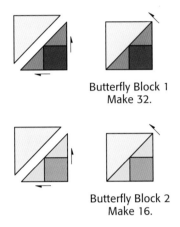

Butterfly Block 1
Make 32.

Butterfly Block 2
Make 16.

2. Sew a 3½" beige square to each of the units made in step 1.

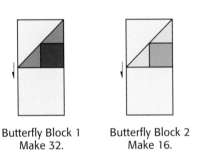

Butterfly Block 1
Make 32.

Butterfly Block 2
Make 16.

3. Join matching units made in step 2 to make Butterfly blocks 1 and 2.

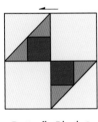 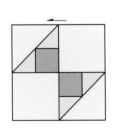

Butterfly Block 1
Make 16.

Butterfly Block 2
Make 8.

Flower Blocks

1. Sew a 4¼" orange triangle to a 4¼" beige triangle; add a red triangle. Sew a 4¼" yellow triangle to a 4¼" beige triangle; add a medium gold triangle.

Flower Block 1
Make 8.

Flower Block 2
Make 8.

2. Sew two 2⅜" beige triangles to each 4¼" orange triangle. Sew two 2⅜" beige triangles to each 4¼" yellow triangle.

Flower Block 1
Make 8.

Flower Block 2
Make 8.

3. Join matching units made in steps 1 and 2.

Flower Block 1
Make 8.

Flower Block 2
Make 8.

4. Sew two 2" × 5" beige rectangles to each unit.

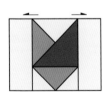 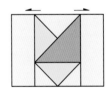

Flower Block 1
Make 8.

Flower Block 2
Make 8.

5. Sew a 2⅜" beige triangle to each 2⅜" medium green triangle. Join 2 triangle units, a 1¼" × 2" green piece, and two 1⅝" × 2" beige pieces.

Make 32.

Make 16.

6. Join the units made in steps 4 and 5 to complete Flower blocks 1 and 2.

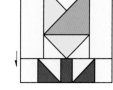

Flower Block 1
Make 8.

Flower Block 2
Make 8.

Assembly and Finishing

1. Arrange the blocks as shown. Sew the blocks into horizontal rows, then join the rows.

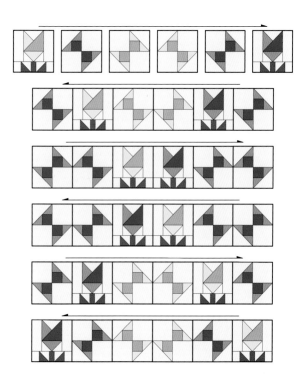

2. Sew the side inner border strips to the quilt top. Sew Flower blocks to each end of the remaining inner border strips, then add these to the top and bottom edges.

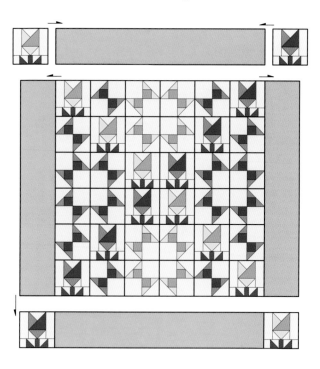

3. Sew outer border strips to the sides of the quilt top, then to the top and bottom edges.

4. Referring to "Assembly and Finishing" on pages 91–96, layer your quilt top with batting and backing; baste. Quilt as desired, bind the edges, and make a label for your quilt.

Assembly and Finishing

JOINING BLOCKS

Arrange the blocks as shown in the project illustrations. The layout stage is your last opportunity to move blocks around before joining them. To get a perspective on the design and the color placement, look at your quilt through a camera lens. You might see something through the lens that stands out and needs to be addressed. Let me warn you not to play too much with moving the blocks around. If you are an organized person, you might be tempted to organize the blocks in some kind of sequence. Try to avoid doing this—remember, it's the random play of fabrics that makes stash quilts interesting.

Sew the blocks in rows, pressing the seam allowances in opposite directions from row to row so they will "lock" in place when you stitch them together. Join the rows. Press the seams in one direction. Don't forget to machine baste any matching points (see the Tip on page 23).

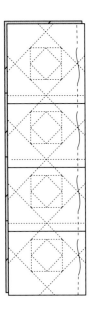

ADDING BORDERS

The quilts in this book are made either with borders with straight-cut corners or borders with corner squares. If multiple borders are added, follow these directions, incorporating the previous border as part of the quilt top.

Borders with Straight-Cut Corners

1. Measure the length of the quilt top at the center, from raw edge to raw edge, and cut 2 border strips to match that measurement. Mark the centers of the border strips and the sides of the quilt top. Join the borders to the sides, matching center marks and edges and easing as necessary. Press the seam allowances toward the borders.

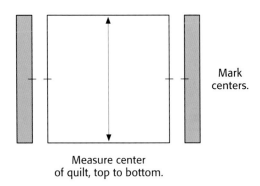

Mark centers.

Measure center of quilt, top to bottom.

2. Measure the width of the quilt top through the center from raw edge to raw edge, including the border pieces just added. Cut 2 border strips to match that measurement. Mark the centers of the border strips and the top and bottom of the quilt top. Join the border strips to the top and bottom edges, matching centers and ends and easing as necessary. Press the seams toward the borders.

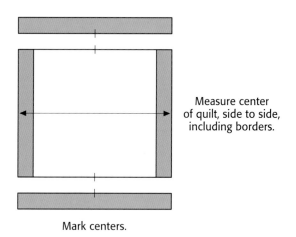

Measure center of quilt, side to side, including borders.

Mark centers.

Borders with Corner Squares

1. Measure all 4 border strips before adding side borders, as described for borders with straight-cut corners. Sew border strips to the sides of the quilt top, and press the seam allowances toward the borders.
2. Sew the corner squares to the top and bottom borders and press the seams toward the borders. Sew the borders to the top and bottom edges of the quilt top, matching the corner-square seams with the side border seams.

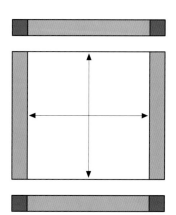

REMOVING THE PAPER

If you paper-pieced your quilt, it is now time to remove the paper. Gently tug on the block from corner to corner and side to side to pull the paper away from the stitching. This is something you can do while watching TV or talking on the phone as it is a pretty mindless activity.

BACKING AND BATTING

To create a backing for your quilt, cut two lengths of fabric, the length of the quilt plus about 4". Remove the selvages from both lengths. Sew the pieces together with a $1/4$"-wide seam allowance, or split one piece lengthwise and sew the resulting pieces to either side of the other length. Press the seam allowances open.

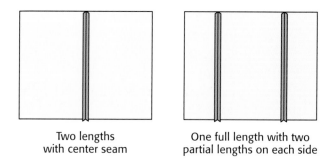

Two lengths with center seam

One full length with two partial lengths on each side

Cut the batting to the size of the quilt top plus another 2" to 4".

TIP

The backing is another opportunity to use fabric from your stash. You can piece several different fabrics to make a backing for your quilt, so long as it is large enough to cover the back of the quilt plus approximately 4" extra all around.

BASTING

To baste the backing, batting, and quilt top together:

1. Spread the backing, wrong side up, on a clean surface. You can use the floor or a table, depending on the size of the project. Being careful not to stretch the backing out of shape, anchor it to your work surface. If you're working on a carpet, use pins; if you're working on a hard surface, use masking tape.
2. Spread and smooth the batting over the backing, making sure it covers evenly.
3. Center the quilt top on the batting, right side up, smoothing out any wrinkles. Make sure the edges of the quilt top are parallel to the edges of the backing.
4. If you plan to hand quilt, begin basting from the center to the outside edge. Make vertical and horizontal rows of basting stitches about 5" to 8" apart and two diagonal rows from corner to corner.

   If you plan to machine quilt, pin-baste from the center to the outside edge, using size 1 or 2 rustproof safety pins and placing them about 4" apart.

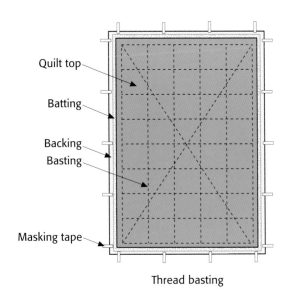

Quilt top

Batting

Backing

Basting

Masking tape

Thread basting

5. Bring the edge of the back over the edge of the exposed batting and baste to the top of the quilt.

QUILTING

The quilts in this book can be hand quilted, machine quilted, or a combination of both. Save intricate quilting designs for open areas where they can be appreciated. Begin quilting in the middle of the quilt and work toward the outside edges in a consistent fashion.

ADDING A SLEEVE

If you plan to hang the quilt, you will want to baste the raw edges of a sleeve to the quilt before adding the binding.

1. Cut a strip of fabric as long as the width of the quilt and double the desired depth of the sleeve plus an additional 1/2" for seam allowances. Hem both ends of the strip.

2. Fold the strip wrong sides together, and pin the raw edges at the top of the quilt before you attach the binding. Machine baste in place, 1/8" from the edge. Add the binding to the quilt.

3. Blindstitch the folded edge of the sleeve to the back of the quilt.

BINDING

Once the quilting is complete, it's time to bind the quilt. Prepare the quilt by removing any basting stitches and trimming the batting and backing even with the edge of the quilt top. Using a walking foot or an even-feed foot on your sewing machine, sew a basting stitch around the perimeter of the quilt, approximately ⅛" from the edge. The walking foot will help you sew all three layers smoothly. If you are adding a sleeve to hang your quilt project, baste it in place now (see facing page). Because the edges of wall quilts do not receive stress from handling, I prefer to use straight-grain binding on them. When binding bed quilts, I cut fabric strips on the bias because bias strips are stronger.

1. Cut 2"-wide strips across the width of the fabric (crosswise grain) or on the bias, and sew the ends together at a 45° angle to make a strip long enough to go around the perimeter of the quilt, plus about 10". Press the seams open.

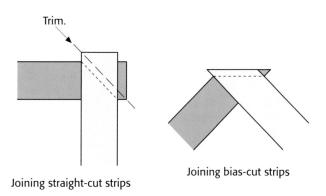

Joining straight-cut strips

Joining bias-cut strips

2. Fold the binding strip in half lengthwise, wrong sides together, and press. Clip the "dog" ears.

To attach the binding:

1. Place the binding strip (either straight grain or bias grain) wrong side up on the cutting mat. Align a rotary ruler's 45° angle marking with the edge of the strip near one end. Draw a "cutting line."

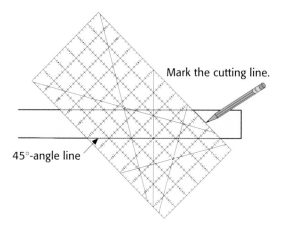

Mark the cutting line.

45°-angle line

Turn the strip and draw 2 more lines, each ¼" from the previous line.

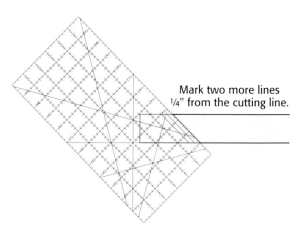

Mark two more lines ¼" from the cutting line.

The first line is the cutting line, the second is the "sewing line" and the third is the "measuring line." Cut on the cutting line.

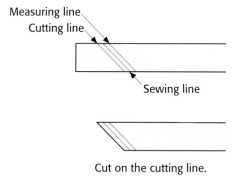

Measuring line
Cutting line
Sewing line

Cut on the cutting line.

2. Fold the strip in half lengthwise, wrong sides together, and press.

3. Place the binding on the front of the quilt, in the middle of the bottom edge, aligning the raw edges of the binding with the edge of the quilt. Attach a walking foot or even-feed foot to your sewing machine. Starting about 6" from the end of the binding, sew the binding to the quilt with a ¼"-wide seam allowance. Stop stitching ¼" from the corner of the quilt and backstitch.

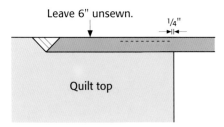

4. Turn the quilt to sew the next edge. Fold the binding up, away from the quilt, and then down, even with the next side. The straight fold should be even with the upper edge of the quilt. Stitch from the edge to the next corner, stopping ¼" from the corner. Repeat for the remaining corners.

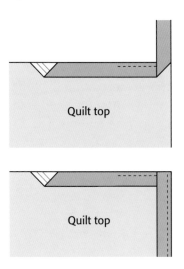

5. After the last corner is stitched, stop. Unfold the strip and place it under the beginning of the binding. On the wrong side, mark the raw edge of the strip at the measuring line on the beginning strip.

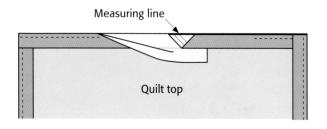

6. Align the rotary ruler's 45°-angle line with the straight edge of the end tail, with the edge of the ruler at the mark. Draw a cutting line. Draw a sewing line ¼" away as shown. Place the binding strip on the cutting table, *away from the quilt*, and cut on the cutting line.

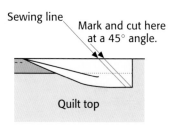

Wrong side of the binding strip

7. Pull the ends of the binding away from the quilt. Place the unfolded strips right sides together as shown. Pin, matching the 2 sewing lines, and stitch. Press the seam allowances open. Clip the "dog ears" and lightly press the strip in half again.

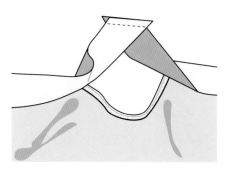

8. Return the strip to the edge of the quilt and finish the seam.

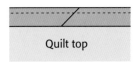

9. Fold the binding to the back, over the raw edges of the quilt. The folded edge of the binding should cover the machine stitching lines. Blindstitch the binding in place.

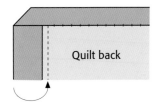 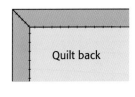

SIGNING YOUR WORK

It's important that you do one more thing to make your quilt complete. That is to make a label for the back of your quilt providing information about you as the maker and the date the quilt was made. The label can be as simple as a piece of fabric or you can make a small patchwork block. Write the information using a permanent pen and attach it to the back of the quilt either before or after quilting. Please don't leave future generations wondering about who made this quilt and when.

Parting Thoughts

For me, writing a quilt book is a way to share something I am excited about. When I began teaching others how to make quilts nearly twenty years ago, I did so because I loved the creative expression patchwork designs offered and couldn't wait to share my excitement and techniques with others.

I've enjoyed sharing how to use stash fabrics to produce dynamic quilts that are fun to make. My friends who made quilts for this book shared the wonder of seeing each slightly different block work in harmony with the others. When you make your first stash quilt, you will have the same thrilling experience!

The abundance of new avenues for creating patchwork never ceases to amaze me. My hope is that you will take these avenues and use them to express your creativity. I've shared my stash quilts and stash quilts made by my friends, and I look forward to seeing yours. Have fun!

Carol

Meet the Author

CAROL DOAK is a best-selling author, popular teacher, and award-winning quiltmaker. She began her teaching career in 1980, in Worthington, Ohio. Carol's teaching has taken her to many cities in the United States and beyond. Her lighthearted approach and ability to teach beginners as well as advanced quilters have earned her high marks and positive comments from workshop participants wherever she travels.

Several books have included Carol's blue-ribbon quilts, including *Great American Quilts 1990* and *The Quilt Encyclopedia*. Carol has been featured in several national quilt magazines, and her quilts have appeared on the covers of *Quilter's Newsletter Magazine, Quilt World, Quilting Today, Ladies Circle Patchwork*, and *McCall's Quilting*.

Carol's students encouraged her to write her first book, *Quiltmaker's Guide: Basics & Beyond*, published in 1992. Her best-selling books, approaching half a million in print, are *Easy Machine Paper Piecing, Easy Paper-Pieced Keepsake Quilts, Easy Mix & Match Machine Paper Piecing, Show Me How to Paper Piece, Easy Reversible Vests, Easy Paper-Pieced Miniature Quilts* and *Your First Quilt Book (or it should be!)*.

Carol lives in Windham, New Hampshire, where she claims the cold winters give her plenty of reason to stockpile a fabric stash for insulation!

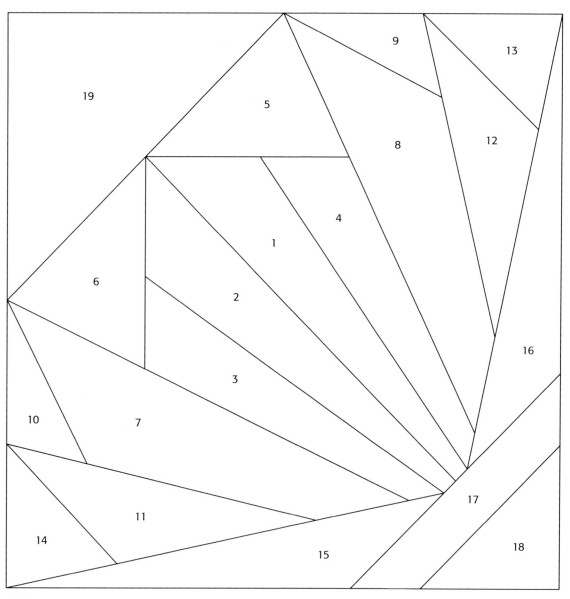

G58

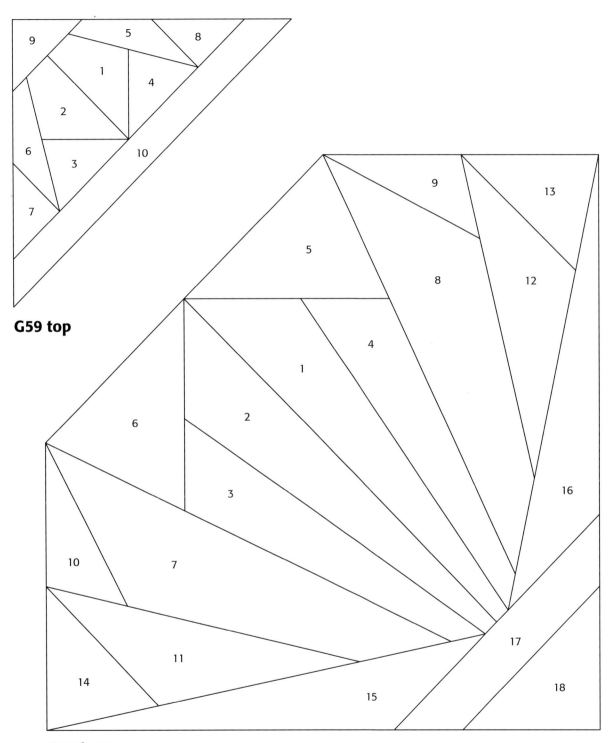

G59 top

G59 bottom

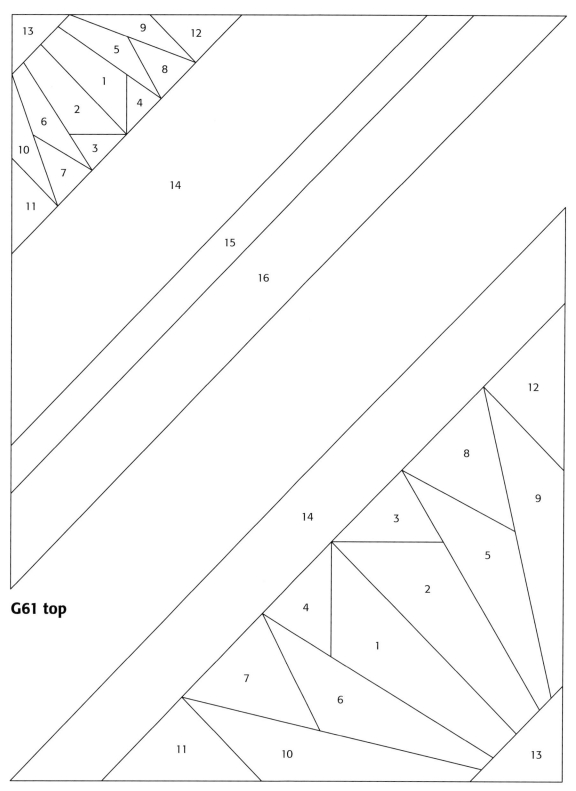

G61 top

G61 bottom

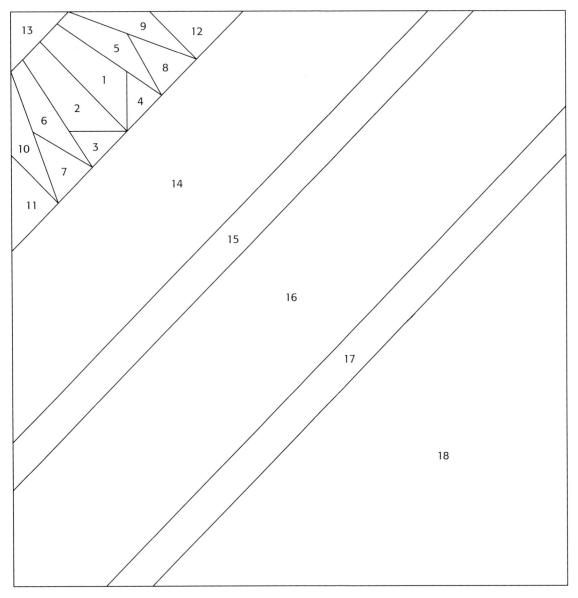

G62

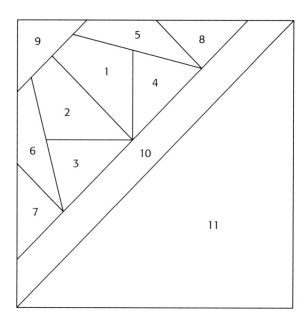

G60

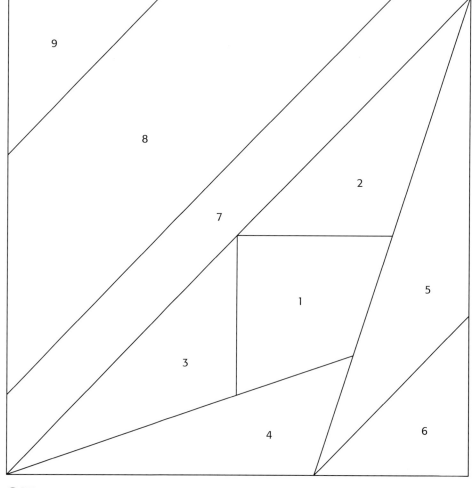

G63

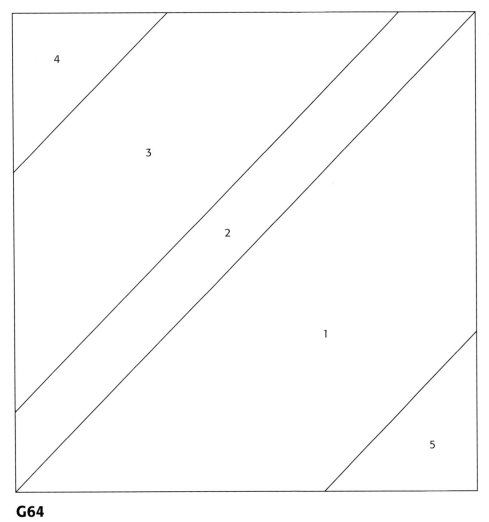

G64

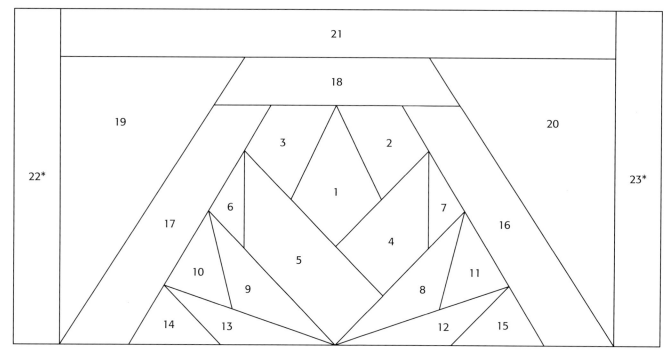

B15 top

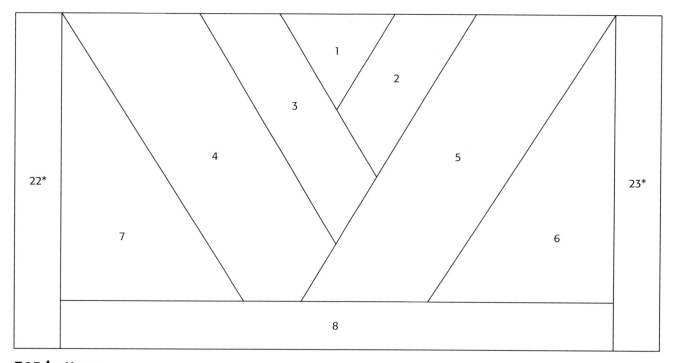

B15 bottom

*Add #22 and #23 after two halves have been joined.

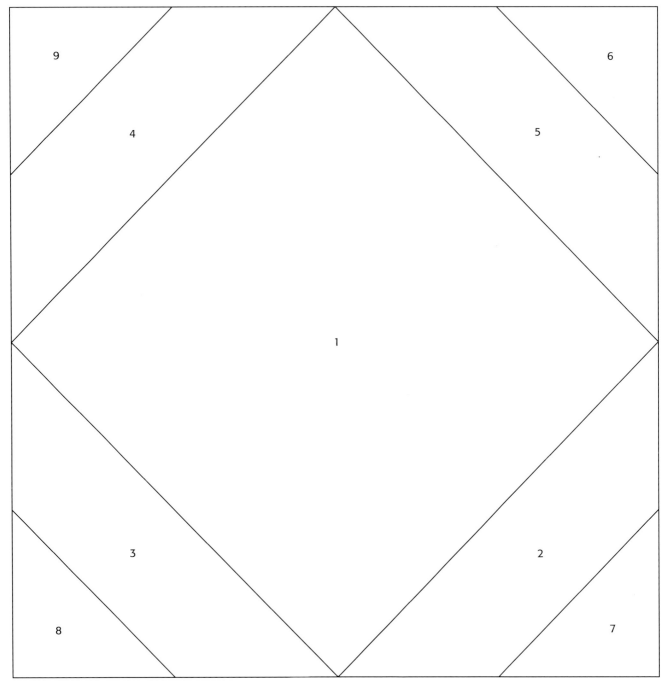

G65

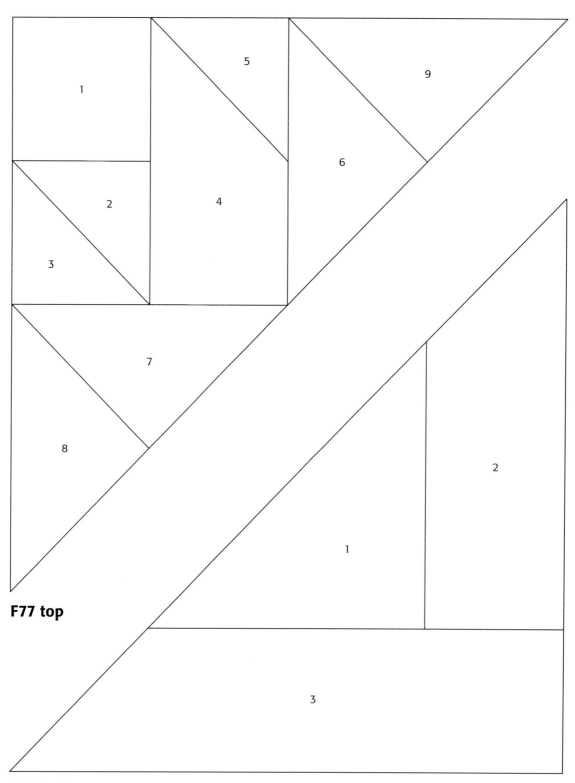

F77 top

F77 bottom

G66

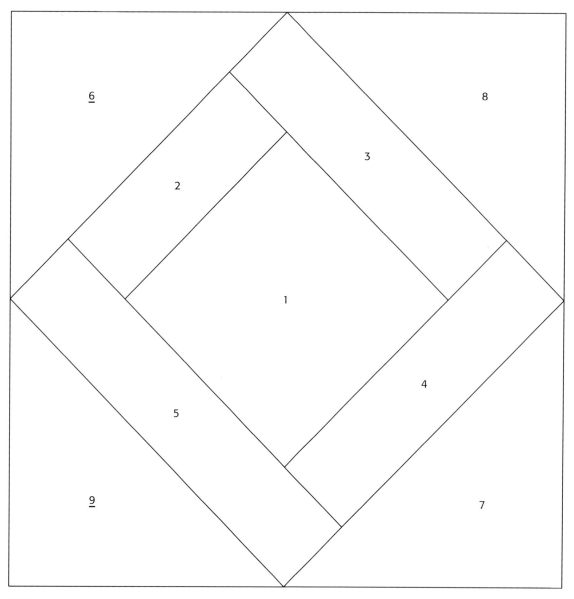

G67

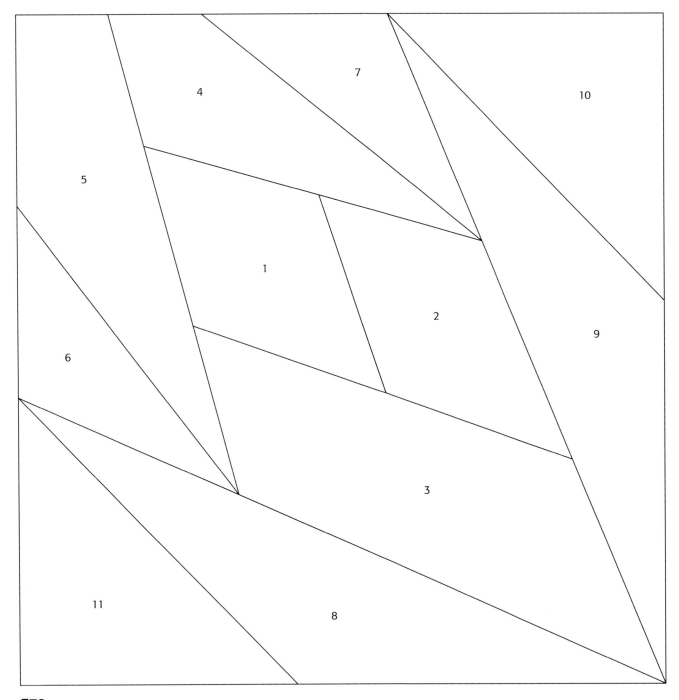

F78

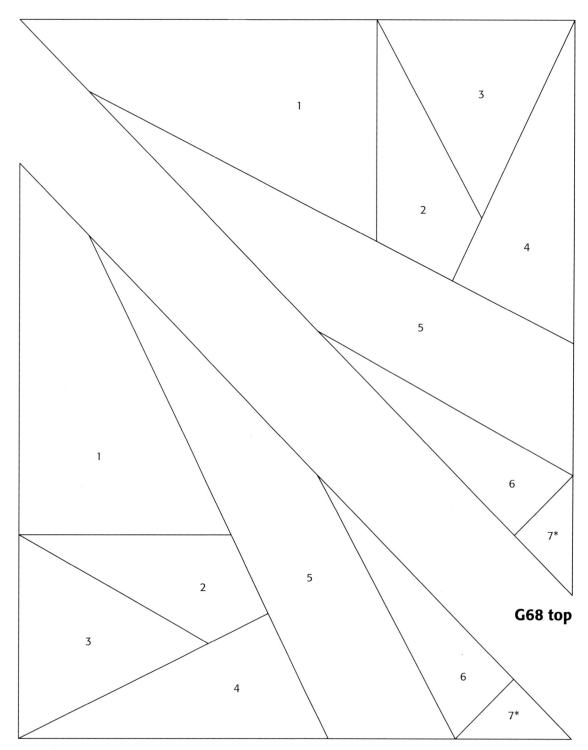

G68 top

G68 bottom

*Add #7 after two halves have been joined.

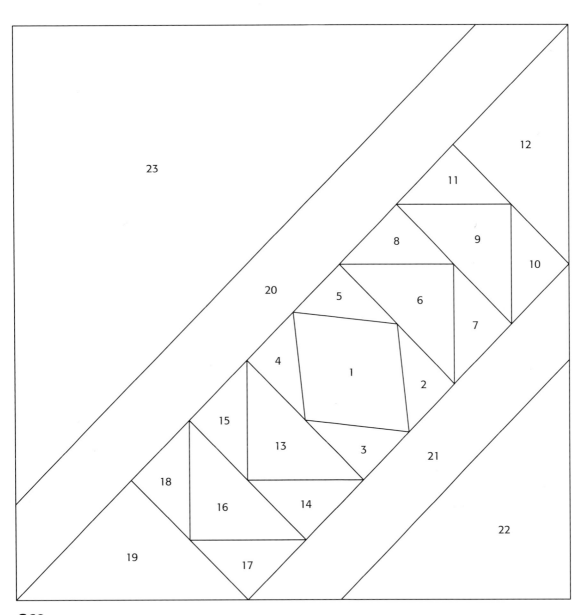

G69

Books and Products from Martingale & Company

Appliqué
Appliqué in Bloom
Baltimore Bouquets
Basic Quiltmaking Techniques for Hand Appliqué
Basic Quiltmaking Techniques for Machine Appliqué
Coxcomb Quilt
The Easy Art of Appliqué
Folk Art Animals
From a Quilter's Garden
Fun with Sunbonnet Sue
Garden Appliqué
Interlacing Borders
Once Upon a Quilt
Stars in the Garden
Sunbonnet Sue All Through the Year
Welcome to the North Pole

Basic Quiltmaking Techniques
Basic Quiltmaking Techniques for Borders & Bindings
Basic Quiltmaking Techniques for Curved Piecing
Basic Quiltmaking Techniques for Divided Circles
Basic Quiltmaking Techniques for Eight-Pointed Stars
Basic Quiltmaking Techniques for Hand Appliqué
Basic Quiltmaking Techniques for Machine Appliqué
Basic Quiltmaking Techniques for Strip Piecing
Your First Quilt Book (or it should be!)

Crafts
15 Beads
The Art of Handmade Paper and Collage
Christmas Ribbonry
Fabric Mosaics
Folded Fabric Fun
Hand-Stitched Samplers from I Done My Best
The Home Decorator's Stamping Book
Making Memories
A Passion for Ribbonry
Stamp with Style

Foundation/Paper Piecing
Classic Quilts with Precise Foundation Piecing
Crazy but Pieceable
Easy Machine Paper Piecing
Easy Mix & Match Machine Paper Piecing
Easy Paper-Pieced Keepsake Quilts
Easy Paper-Pieced Miniatures
Easy Reversible Vests
Foundation Factory Carol Doak Designer Edition
Go Wild with Quilts
Go Wild with Quilts—Again!
It's Raining Cats & Dogs
Mariner's Medallion
Paper Piecing the Seasons
Papers for Foundation Piecing
A Quilter's Ark
Sewing on the Line
Show Me How to Paper Piece

Home Decorating
Decorate with Quilts & Collections
The Home Decorator's Stamping Book
Living with Little Quilts
Make Room for Quilts
Special-Occasion Table Runners
Stitch & Stencil
Welcome Home: Debbie Mumm
Welcome Home: Kaffe Fassett

Joy of Quilting Series
Borders by Design
The Easy Art of Appliqué
A Fine Finish
Hand-Dyed Fabric Made Easy
Happy Endings
Loving Stitches
Machine Quilting Made Easy

A Perfect Match
Press for Success
Sensational Settings
Shortcuts
The Ultimate Book of Quilt Labels

Knitting
Simply Beautiful Sweaters
Two Sticks and a String
Welcome Home: Kaffe Fassett

Machine Quilting/Sewing
Machine Needlelace
Machine Quilting Made Easy
Machine Quilting with Decorative Threads
Quilting Makes the Quilt
Thread Magic
Threadplay

Miniature/Small Quilts
Celebrate! with Little Quilts
Crazy but Pieceable
Easy Paper-Pieced Miniatures
Fun with Miniature Log Cabin Blocks
Little Quilts All Through the House
Living with Little Quilts
Miniature Baltimore Album Quilts
Small Quilts Made Easy
Small Wonders

Quilting/Finishing Techniques
Borders by Design
The Border Workbook
A Fine Finish
Happy Endings
Interlacing Borders
Loving Stitches
Quilt It!
Quilting Design Sourcebook
Quilting Makes the Quilt
Traditional Quilts with Painless Borders
The Ultimate Book of Quilt Labels

Rotary Cutting/Speed Piecing
101 Fabulous Rotary-Cut Quilts
All-Star Sampler
Around the Block with Judy Hopkins
Bargello Quilts
Basic Quiltmaking Techniques for Strip Piecing
Block by Block
Easy Seasonal Wall Quilts
Easy Star Sampler
Fat Quarter Quilts
The Heirloom Quilt
The Joy of Quilting
More Quilts for Baby
More Strip-Pieced Watercolor Magic
A New Slant on Bargello Quilts
A New Twist on Triangles
Patchwork Pantry
Quilters on the Go
Quilting Up a Storm
Quilts for Baby
Quilts from Aunt Amy
ScrapMania
Simply Scrappy Quilts
Square Dance
Strip-Pieced Watercolor Magic
Stripples Strikes Again!
Strips That Sizzle
Two-Color Quilts

Seasonal Projects
Christmas Ribbonry
Easy Seasonal Wall Quilts
Folded Fabric Fun
Holiday Happenings

Quilted for Christmas
Quilted for Christmas, Book III
Quilted for Christmas, Book IV
A Silk-Ribbon Album
Welcome to the North Pole

Stitchery/Needle Arts
Christmas Ribbonry
Crazy Rags
Hand-Stitched Samplers from I Done My Best
Machine Needlelace
Miniature Baltimore Album Quilts
A Passion for Ribbonry
A Silk-Ribbon Album
Victorian Elegance

Surface Design/Fabric Manipulation
15 Beads
The Art of Handmade Paper and Collage
Complex Cloth
Creative Marbling on Fabric
Dyes & Paints
Hand-Dyed Fabric Made Easy
Jazz It Up

Theme Quilts
The Cat's Meow
Everyday Angels in Extraordinary Quilts
Fabric Collage Quilts
Fabric Mosaics
Folded Fabric Fun
Folk Art Quilts
Honoring the Seasons
It's Raining Cats & Dogs
Life in the Country with Country Threads
Making Memories
More Quilts for Baby
The Nursery Rhyme Quilt
Once Upon a Quilt
Patchwork Pantry
Quilted Landscapes
Quilting Your Memories
Quilts for Baby
Quilts from Nature
Through the Window and Beyond
Two-Color Quilts

Watercolor Quilts
More Strip-Pieced Watercolor Magic
Strip-Pieced Watercolor Magic
Watercolor Impressions
Watercolor Quilts

Wearables
Crazy Rags
Dress Daze
Easy Reversible Vests
Jacket Jazz Encore
Just Like Mommy
Variations in Chenille

Many of these books are available through your local quilt, fabric, craft-supply, or art-supply store. For more information, call, write, fax, or e-mail for our free full-color catalog.

Martingale & Company
PO Box 118
Bothell, WA 98041-0118 USA
1-800-426-3126
International: 1-425-483-3313
24-Hour Fax: 1-425-486-7596
Web site: www.patchwork.com
E-mail: info@martingale-pub.com